Public Sociology

Man would not have attained the possible unless time and again he had reached out for the impossible.

—Max Weber

What do they know of sociology, who only sociology know?
—Adapted from C. L. R. James and Rudyard Kipling

For all the students who have taught me so much.

Public Sociology

Between Utopia and Anti-Utopia

Michael Burawoy

polity

Copyright © Michael Burawoy 2021

The right of Michael Burawoy to be identified as Author of this Work has been asserted in accordance with the UK Copyright, Designs and Patents Act 1988.

First published in 2021 by Polity Press

Polity Press
65 Bridge Street
Cambridge CB2 1UR, UK

Polity Press
101 Station Landing
Suite 300
Medford, MA 02155, USA

ISBN-13: 978-1-5095-1914-9
ISBN-13: 978-1-5095-1915-6(pb)

A catalogue record for this book is available from the British Library.

Title: Public sociology : between utopia and anti-utopia / Michael Burawoy.
Description: Cambridge, UK ; Medford, MA : Polity Press, 2021. | Includes bibliographical references and index. | Summary: "Why sociology matters, how sociologists can help the people they study and how it can help us to deal with the crises of the 21st century"-- Provided by publisher.
Identifiers: LCCN 2021006108 (print) | LCCN 2021006109 (ebook) | ISBN 9781509519149 (hardback) | ISBN 9781509519156 (paperback) | ISBN 9781509519187 (epub)
Subjects: LCSH: Sociology.
Classification: LCC HM435 .B87 2021 (print) | LCC HM435 (ebook) | DDC 301--dc23
LC record available at https://lccn.loc.gov/2021006108
LC ebook record available at https://lccn.loc.gov/2021006109

Typeset in 11 on 13pt Sabon
by Fakenham Prepress Solutions, Fakenham, Norfolk NR21 8NL
Printed and bound in Great Britain by CPI Group (UK) Ltd, Croydon

For further information on Polity, visit our website:
politybooks.com

Contents

Tables

Preface

To the 1960s generation sociology promised so much – addressing questions of social justice, social inequality, social movements, and social change. Its potential was famously captured by the American sociologist C. Wright Mills in his definition of sociology as turning "personal troubles" into "public issues." This proves to be easier said than done.

In the chapters that follow I explore the promise of sociology by tracing my own trajectory into and through the discipline. I set out for India in 1967 with the naïve view that sociology would fix social problems if only we have adequate knowledge based on rigorous research. We just have to inform policy makers and they will do the right thing. I call this species of sociology *policy sociology*. My first lesson in sociology was to learn the importance of the social, political, and economic context of decision-making. Recognizing the limits of this policy sociology led me to *public sociology*, which did not speak to policy makers. It transmitted the result of research to broad publics. Here, again, I was naïve, overlooking the operation of power within the public sphere that repressed, diverted, or co-opted the aims of public sociology. That was my second lesson – a lesson I learned in newly independent Zambia from 1968 to 1972.

Instead of giving up on sociology, I decided I didn't have an adequate grasp of its intricacies and its underlying theory. I left Zambia for the PhD program at the University of Chicago. There I discovered that the material I was expected to learn and absorb, what I call *professional sociology*, was more concerned with preserving rather than changing the status quo – or changing it only to keep it the same. So my third lesson concerned the umbilical cord connecting professional sociology to ideology, its complacent adjustment to ubiquitous exploitation, domination, and dispossession. I was not the only one to be disappointed. I became part of a rising generation that advanced a *critical sociology*, critical of the world but also of the reigning professional sociology.

That was the 1970s, when critical sociology was gaining adherents in many universities, not just in the US but across the globe. After graduating from Chicago, through an unlikely succession of events, I landed in the Department of Sociology at the University of California, Berkeley. There the struggle between insurgent graduate students and divided faculty had been particularly intense. After six tumultuous years I survived a tenure battle by the skin of my teeth. During the 1980s, now with the security of tenure, I sought to contribute to an emergent Marxist research program that led me to explore the meaning and possibilities of socialism in Hungary and then in the Soviet Union. I had hardly begun research in the Soviet Union when it collapsed, turning into a crony capitalism that sought to wipe out its "communist" past. Witnessing the inevitable dénouement, what I would call *involution*, I felt helpless and ineffectual. My fourth lesson was the marginality of sociology to ongoing debates.

Disillusioned with my research, facing a backlash against Marxism, I was in retreat when my journey took an unexpected turn. It was 1996. Desperate for

a new chair, my colleagues promoted me from departmental pariah to department head. From there I became
head of the American Sociological Association and then
head of the International Sociological Association. I had
become a professional sociologist par excellence. I used
these platforms to once again project the idea of public
sociology.

Now I saw more clearly how public sociology depended
on the three other knowledges – professional, policy
and critical – if it was to create a conversation between
sociologists and publics concerning the devastation of
society. Drawing on my experiences in Russia I advanced
theories of what has come to be known as neoliberalism,
what I call *third-wave marketization*, how the world
has been subjected to a destructive commodification of
labor, nature, money, and knowledge. I searched for
counter-tendencies, counter-movements that might avert
the catastrophes that lay around the corner. I sought to
understand how the commodification of knowledge was
degrading the university – a vital source of alternative
futures. With a better sense of the context and a more
focused vision of what might be changed, I claimed to
better understand the possibilities of public sociology –
both its production and its reception. An evangelist for
public sociology, I determined that teaching was my own
immediate contribution to public sociology.

This is how I now make sense of my successive experiences as a sociologist, but those experiences emerged
through a quite concrete research journey. If I began my
initiation in 1967 in India, studying university education,
for the next thirty-five years I became an intermittent
worker – a "participant observer" of industry in Zambia,
the US, Hungary, and Russia. My training as an anthropologist in Zambia led me to study others by joining them
in their lives, that is, in their space and in their time. It
meant that I became an unskilled worker in factories,
helping to produce (and sometimes ruin) engines, gear
boxes, steel, and furniture – my incompetence being an

embarrassment and often a danger to myself and my fellow workers. I traced the lived experience on the shop floor to the wider political, economic, and social realms. I demonstrated how my experience in the Zambian mining industry expressed the transition to postcolonialism, how my experience in the Chicago branch of Allis-Chalmers reflected the physiognomy of advanced capitalism, how my experience in the auto industry and steel industries of Hungary carried the dynamics of state socialism, and how my experience in rubber and furniture plants in the Soviet Union was shaped by the demise of state socialism and the transition to capitalism. My professional life was enlivened by a continuing struggle to defend the legitimacy of such an extension from micro-processes to macro-forces, but such an extension is the necessary foundation of any public sociology, for turning those personal troubles into public issues.

Since beginning this critical memoir five years ago I have lost my close friend Erik Olin Wright. He was a constant companion in the reconstruction of Marxism, what we were to call *sociological Marxism*. Technically, we were sociologists, rooted in the sociology departments that recruited us in 1976 – he at the University of Wisconsin–Madison and I at the University of California, Berkeley. Undeniably our professional commitments made us sociologists, but we were Marxist sociologists committed to the advance of sociological Marxism, a Marxism that restored the *social* in socialism. We had set out to supplant sociology, showing that Marxist science was superior to sociology. Over time we diluted our grandiose schemes but without ever losing our commitment to Marxism.

Erik moved from a scientific Marxism focused on "class analysis" to a critical Marxism focused on "real utopias," discovering the rudiments of socialist principles in the interstices and dynamics of capitalism. He scoured the globe for such concrete manifestations of an alternative world, collaborating with activists and practitioners to connect these different experiments and struggles. He became a public sociologist. He will, perhaps, be best remembered for his last two books, both appearing posthumously. The first is a manifesto for real utopias, *How To Be an Anticapitalist in the 21st Century* (2019) – a popular version of his magnum opus, *Envisioning Real Utopias* (2010). The manifesto was instantly translated into thirteen languages, a reflection of his enormous influence not just in academia but among activists fighting for a better world. The second book, *Stardust to Stardust* (2020), is an extraordinary daily journal of reflections on living and dying. It begins in April 2018 when Erik was diagnosed with acute myeloid leukemia, and ends nine months later with his death. Always one to live for the future, Erik showed us how to sustain optimism in the face of both personal and human extinctions. The book radiates utopianism not just in theory but also in practice: it relates how he turned life around him – family, neighborhood, school, department, and hospital – into a real utopia. His spirit guides this memoir, continuing the explorations that we began together – the tensions between utopia and anti-utopia.

Although I have acknowledged my teachers many times before, I would be remiss if I did not acknowledge them once again. In their different ways Jaap van Velsen, who died in 1990, Adam Przeworski, and Bill Wilson made indelible imprints on me and my intellectual outlook. But I have had so many other teachers, too. My friends from South Africa, especially Eddie Webster, Luli Callinicos, and Harold Wolpe, who died in 1996, continually reminded me that another world exists, one of hope and struggle. My Hungarian and Russian escapades would not have been possible were it not for friends, colleagues, and collaborators, especially Iván Szelényi, János Lukács, Zsuzsa Hunyadi, Pavel Krotov, Tatyana Lytkina, Svetlana Yaroshenko, Volodya Ilyin, and Marina Ilyina, who inducted me into the byzantine world of socialism and postsocialism. Elsewhere, thanks to Shen Yuan who guided me through China, to Ruy Braga for introducing me to

Brazil, to Nazanin Shahrokni for giving me an unforgettable glimpse of Iran, to Sari Hanafi who showed me so many different sides of Lebanon, Jordan, and Palestine, and to Mona Abaza for walking me through Cairo's urban life during and after the Arab Spring. In England and in Wales, Huw Beynon has been a close friend, ever since we met to discuss industrial ethnography in a dark Chicago bar in 1975. I'm grateful to so many others in so many countries who have helped me understand how sociology contributes to making a better world.

The influence of students, both undergraduates and graduate students, has been deep, incalculable, and irreversible, not just in educating me but in making me, as I like to think, a better person. One former student, Laleh Behbehanian, now a brilliant teacher in Berkeley's sociology department, became the driving force behind this project. She became my coach. Her enthusiasm helped to dilute my skepticism concerning the value of my sociological account of my sociological life. She read the manuscript three times; each time her detailed comments sent me scurrying back to revise the manuscript. I was getting a dose of my own medicine. After the fourth iteration I couldn't bear to give it to her again. Enough already!

Besides, I was exhausting the patience of my editor at Polity, Pascal Porcheron, who had first approached me to write a short introduction to sociology. I originally agreed in the hope that I could write something for the undergraduates I had been teaching for 40 years. I owed them so much. It soon became apparent I was incapable of such an introduction. Instead I developed a reflection on my own trajectory through the four sociologies I had elaborated as president of the American Sociological Association in 2004 – the matrix of policy, public, critical, and professional sociologists. Unhappy with the drafts I sent him, I would have junked the whole enterprise were it not for the generous comments of two anonymous reviewers, as well as encouraging suggestions from Pascal himself who read

it not once but twice. They had found value in my reflections, so I continued in what seemed to me a Sisyphean
task. I also benefited from the suggestions of Chris Muller
on Chapter 10 and of Chris Newfield on Chapter 15.
With Tyler Leeds's meticulous corrections and pointed
suggestions, I was able to push the manuscript over the hill
and into the abyss below. Ann Klefstad's careful editing
delivered the final touch.

William Faulkner famously wrote, "The past is never
dead. It's not even past," yet still the past is understood
differently with time. Even in the last five years my views
have evolved in unexpected ways. It could not be otherwise
as I struggled to complete this little book in the midst of
COVID-19 – a mounting health and economic crisis –
not to mention police atrocities, insurgent movements
on left and right, and Trumpian megalomania. From the
perspective of Oakland, California, it looks like the planet
will never be the same again. The pandemic has exposed
the deepening inequalities and suffering that sociologists
have been studying for decades. But COVID-19 has not
just exposed those inequalities, it has amplified them. This
should be a time when sociology comes into its own, as
the crisis compels everyone to adopt a sociological vision;
sociology shows us how capitalism can be defenseless
against the accumulating crises it nurtures. But the state
response, the social protest against anti-Black policing, the
successful struggle against Trumpism, and the strategies of
human coping have opened up new possibilities, new imaginations of what the world could be like, should be like,
has to be like, if it is to contain global pandemics, climate
change, and racial injustice. Sociology's utopian mission
remains making those possibilities real, an endeavour that
also depends on recognizing what an uphill struggle that
will be. But, as Erik Wright used to say, optimistically,
"Where there's a way there's a will."

Introduction
The Promise of Sociology

It was 1967. I was sitting in Christ's College Library, very depressed. I was a grammar school boy who didn't belong in such a citadel of learning. I resented Cambridge – its spires and its gardens, its rituals and its gowns, its dons and its curfews, all things passed down from time immemorial. I resented the mathematics I was there to study, so removed from the world beyond. The place, the subject, the atmosphere all seemed so irrelevant, so meaningless.

And there on the desk, next to me, appeared a book called *Suicide*. That must be for me, I thought – a recipe for a way out of my misery. I picked it up and started reading. It was a strange tome written by some Frenchman called Émile Durkheim. As far as I could tell this turgid text made an astonishing claim: suicide – that most individual of acts, committed in a state of desperation – was a product of something beyond the individual, namely, the social relations one inhabits.

Rates of suicide, the propensity to commit suicide, Durkheim (1897) showed, varied with the group or society to which one belonged. Social relations that encourage excessive individualism lead to *egoistic* suicide. So Protestants, he claimed, are more likely to commit suicide than Catholics, men more than women. Group relations that demand exacting conformity, as in military units or in societies with strict moral codes, can cause *altruistic* suicide, the opposite of egoistic suicide. States of moral confusion – when life loses its meaning, when people experience rapid social mobility, or when society is in crisis – lead to *anomic* suicide. So, there it was, I was suffering from anomie. Ironically, *Suicide* healed my depression far better than any pill or even psychotherapy. Far from offering a road to ending my life, *Suicide* would inspire a lifelong commitment to sociology. This was sociotherapy based on socioanalysis.

To know that what we do is limited by forces outside our immediate control can be paralyzing but it can also be strangely liberating, as the pressures on the self are redirected to the world beyond, a world we share with others. As Karl Marx, another sociologist, once wrote: we make history, but not under conditions of our own choosing. This is the defining question of sociology: How do human beings make their worlds under external constraints? Sociology discovers what those constraints are, but not only that. In addition, sociology studies how those constraints may be changed to expand the realm of possibilities.

Sociology excavates the often-repressed desire for a different world, a better world, and explores the conditions of and obstacles to its realization. Sociology is caught between the possible and the impossible: between the *utopian imagination* reaching beyond the constraints on human action and the *anti-utopian science* that reveals their existence and power. By "anti-utopian" I don't mean "dystopian," which refers to an undesirable or "bad" society, but the limits on the realization of a "good" society.

There are three moments to utopian thinking. First, there is the simple desire for a better world, the originating impulse that impels us to become sociologists. We become sociologists not to become rich but to make a better world, whatever *better* might mean – more equal, more free, more cooperative. Second, those values form the basis of a systematic critique of society, the way the realization of values are systematically obstructed – how inequality, domination, egoism are reproduced by the social institutions we inhabit. This is the anti-utopian moment. Third, those same values can be molded into a vision of an alternative world. These alternatives are not blueprints; they are provisional, experimental, and tentative. In principle, they have nothing to do with totalitarianism and everything to do with emancipation. In this final moment the utopian imagination is not an abstract design but an elaboration, a one-sided elaboration of actually existing institutions, organizations, what Erik Wright called "real utopias," what Max Weber called "ideal-types." Suspended between their utopian aspirations and anti-utopian constraints, sociologists become archeologists excavating the world for emancipatory possibilities, now and in the past, here and there.[1] The sociologist is impelled to discover the embryos of alternative worlds by an incessant lament directed at the existing world.

Given Cambridge's insulation from the world beyond, it is not surprising that sociology never took root on such infertile soil. Other disciplines have thrived within such insulation: anthropology as the study of the colonial other as though it were a permanent fixture; economics as the fabrication of abstract models, removed from human experience; moral philosophy as the study of universal injunctions. They had long traditions in Cambridge. But sociology – this Johnny-come-lately discipline, flourishing in the red-brick universities at the time – was taboo. Sociology's crass descent into abject lives threatened the sacred distance of scholarly endeavor. Sociology invites everyone – scholars, students, and lay-people – to reflect on the social world in which *they* dwell as a condition of comprehending the world in which others dwell. It compels the recognition, and takes as its principle assumption and challenge, that we are part of the world we study – participants in the world we observe or observers in the world in which we participate. We are not above the world; we are in the world. There's no knowledge from nowhere.

Still, this poses a problem – how can we study the world as we participate in it? We need some stabilizing rudder that will guide us through the swamps of society. This brings us back to the discipline's founding values. Sociology is a science that is built on moral commitment, on values that we hold deeply with others – freedom, reason, equality, solidarity. Different sociologists hold different values, but some value or set of values is necessary to stabilize our exploration of the world of which we are a part. This guided exploration, this science, seeks out the forces that obstruct the realization of what we value – forces that are hidden but, all the more certainly, govern our world. If everything were transparent to the actor, then there would be no science. We are in search of the invisible so as to make it visible – and thus more mutable – to ourselves and to others.

It is not enough to defend values in the abstract. A sociological approach to values is to discover them as embedded in institutions – institutions that incubate values as utopian imaginations that prefigure an alternative world. They might be the workplace free of alienation, the family free of domination, education free of inequality. The external forces we explore are the anti-utopian limits on the realization of those utopias. But these limits are not immoveable. As Max Weber writes in the epigraph to this book – the realization of the possible is through the pursuit of the impossible. Or to put it slightly differently, the pursuit of the impossible shifts the limits of the possible. To expand them we have to identify them and understand them. If we are not careful, however, the pursuit of the impossible can restrict as well expand those limits. Here lies the tragic moment of sociology – the way it maps the unintended consequences of utopian strivings. Without attention to the anti-utopian science, utopian strivings can, indeed, turn into dystopian nightmares.

It took me a few decades to come to these conclusions: to recognize the meaning of sociology as a value-based science, rooted in lived experience and focused on the tension between utopian and anti-utopian thinking. This book relates that process of discovery. It is not a novel, however. So it begins with my point of arrival. Part One begins by describing the utopian and anti-utopian tensions that lie at the heart of sociology as read through the conventional classics of sociology – Marx, Weber, and Durkheim – but captured most clearly in the life and writings of W. E. B. Du Bois. Feminists have made their own distinctive contributions.

The classics are also the founders of sociology because they had to carve out the distinctiveness of sociology as against other disciplines – psychology, economics, philosophy, history, and even theology – while at the same time drawing on them. Over the last century (and this is the subject of the second chapter), sociology has advanced as an academic discipline with its own division of labor, often trying to shed those founders either because they are obstacles to the progress of "value-free" science or because they are mired in the prejudices of their time. The classics are classics, however, because they transcend their time: they speak to the crises we face and are rooted in values we embrace. Their time is still our time.

Part Two turns to the point of departure, starting where so many of us begin – with policy sociology's naïve view that social problems have technical solutions. I went to India in the earnest belief that the question as to which language should be the medium of instruction in Indian universities could be solved by what today would be called a *field experiment*. I came away understanding that wider political and economic context interests were the major contributors to any solution. I thought that integrating Black and white pay scales in the copper industry of postcolonial Zambia was a mathematical problem, but I quickly learned that the supposedly neutral job evaluation scheme I constructed already contained within it a solution defined by the preexisting racial order. I had entered the realm of policy sociology driven by utopian desire but without anti-utopian science.

Part Three, therefore, recognizes the limits to social change, leading me to public sociology and the hope that stimulating public debate and the exercise of collective rationality could shift those limits. Thus, television and print media disseminated the results of our study of the persistence of the color bar in the Zambian copper mines. Yet dissemination was not enough. Even though the study engendered public debate, the multinational corporation was able to deploy the results in its own interests. Casting one's findings into the public sphere that is populated by powerful actors can have unexpected and unintended consequences – often unfavorable consequences. Thus, I turned from this traditional, mediated public sociology, to what I call an organic public sociology – an intimate, organic connection between sociologists and their constituency. I worked with students at the University of Zambia to collectively contest government policies. But this, too, was diverted into a losing political battle. In another continent – Latin America – these interventions might be called *participant action research*, which had its own fateful consequences, including the disappearance of sociology.

Despairing, I realized I simply understood too little of the forces shaping the outcomes of these public interventions – the unintended consequences of intentional action. Part Four follows my path as a graduate student to the University of Chicago, one of the historic heartlands of sociology. I was very disappointed by what was on offer – a parochial and self-referential vision of sociology. I took up arms against this professional sociology in critiques of extant theories of race, of development, and then of work – theories that served racial domination, neocolonialism, and capitalist profit. I turned against those reigning theories and their comforting illusions: that racism would simply evaporate through assimilation; that Third World countries released from colonialism would take off into modernity; that pretending to treat workers as human beings would get them to work harder. When the illusions proved to be just that, illusions, the temptation was to blame the victims – pathologized people of color, tradition-oriented colonized, lazy workers. Instead I drew on an anti-utopian Marxist research program to interrogate the class character of racial orders, the reproduction of cheap labor power through migration, and what I called "the politics of production." I remain committed to participant observation, studying the factory I worked in, challenging the objectivity of the removed scholar, and gaining insight into the subjectivity of industrial labor. At the end of this part I bring together the ideas of the preceding chapters to assess one important sociological framework for studying race as it applied to South Africa. Together these four chapters in Part Four comprise *critical sociology* – a critique of the world but also of professional sociology as it was then.

Part Five describes my own trajectory into professional sociology. It opens with a series of flukes that landed me a position at Berkeley. This was as radical a department of sociology as you could find in the US, but it was still driven by the imperatives of the discipline. To survive I had to develop a research program – both a methodology and a theory – that could advance Marxism within professional sociology. What was at stake was not only the advance of a Marxist science, not only my own survival, but also securing jobs for my students. To establish some sort of legitimacy for Marxism I had to respond to mainstream critics of my research. Among other things, they were skeptical of the generality of my claims based on the study of a single factory. They doubted that my experiences in my Chicago factory were a function of capitalism rather than modern industrialism. I responded by developing the "extended case method" but also turning, once again, to working in factories, this time in socialist Hungary. There I identified their specifically socialist organization

of labor, their specifically socialist production politics, and
how they harbored a real utopia of democratic socialism.
There were similarities between socialist and capitalist
production, but there were also fundamental differences.

History took an unexpected turn. In 1989, while I was
working away in the Lenin Steel Works (LKM), then the
biggest and oldest steel mill in Hungary, state socialism
crumbled. The democratic socialism I had envisioned from
within the furnaces of LKM was never a serious contender;
instead state socialism gave way to a destructive capitalism.
That transition was not what I had come to Hungary to
study. So I migrated to the still-standing high command of
state socialism, to become a worker in the Soviet Union.
But not for long. It was 1991 and the Soviet Union was
itself in flux, about to sink into an extortionate merchant
capitalism. From their lofty perch the Western economists
were debating whether the transition to capitalism should
be a *revolutionary* break with communism (shock therapy)
or an *evolutionary* movement built through the creation
of new supportive institutions. From where I was, in the
factory, all I could see was the post-Soviet economy's
self-destructive *involution*. The realm of exchange was
flourishing but it came at the cost of production – out
of the planned economy arose barter, mafia, and banks
eating away at industry and agriculture. A few were
making enormous gains, while the vast majority sank into
precarity. Utopian thinking – mine as well as theirs – was
dashed, once again, on unseen rocks.

With no factories to work in, I followed the fate of
my fellow workers as they wrestled with what I called
"primitive disaccumulation," the wanton destruction of
the Soviet economy. This widespread faith in market
fundamentalism – as though capitalism would spring
spontaneously from the ruins of communism, as though
there was a market road to a market economy – required
a shift of critical perspective from Karl Marx to Karl
Polanyi, taking Marxism in new directions. Karl Polanyi's
The Great Transformation (1944), a classic treatise on the

dangers of overextending the market, reconstructed *The Communist Manifesto* for the twentieth century, shifting the focus of attention from production to exchange, from exploitation to commodification, from the state to society, from class struggle to the counter-movement. In its account of market ideology as well as market reality, Polanyi's theory fitted the transition from socialism to capitalism far better than Marx. But it was a depressing scene, with people struggling for survival and with no better future in sight.

My sociology seemed irrelevant, impotent, but it was given new energy from the place I least expected. Part Six opens with the strange circumstances that led to my ascent up the professional ladder, into the leadership of national and international sociological associations. From that perch I returned to the quest for public sociology, inspired by the work of my colleagues and students at Berkeley, but also drawn to the committed sociology of South Africa driven by the fight against apartheid. I now understood that the advance of public sociology required an understanding of the world it sought to engage as well as the conditions of knowledge production.

The post-Soviet transition – not a "great transformation" but a "great involution" – accelerated "neoliberalism," deepening what I call *third-wave marketization* that has left no part of the world untouched. What I experienced in Russia during the 1990s was an exaggerated, pathological form of anarchic capitalism, dominated by finance, that has spread across the world. State socialism as the actually existing alternative to capitalism had dissolved, and with it the utopian variants it harbored. It now became necessary to search for socialist alternatives within the interstices of capitalism.

With a Polanyian lens I could see how third-wave marketization threatened human existence, and, at the same time, paralyzed liberal democracy, giving rise to right-wing and left-wing populisms as well as to authoritarian regimes. The counter-movements to first- and second-wave marketization in the nineteenth and twentieth centuries developed their own utopias, but the counter-movement to third-wave marketization seemed bereft of a utopian dimension, in large part because of the discrediting of the idea of socialism. One task for sociology today is to advance such utopian visions.

But is sociology capable of such visions? To answer that question, I turn to the conditions for the production of knowledge, not least the university, which is itself not exempt from the invading forces of capitalism. Third-wave marketization enters the university through the commodification of the production and dissemination of knowledge, which sets in motion a succession of crises: fiscal crisis, governance crisis, identity crisis, and legitimation crisis. If there was any doubt, this transformation of the university is the living demonstration that we are part of the world we study. It is no longer possible, if it ever was, to hold on to notions of sociology assembled from outside the world it studies. The university can no longer be conceived of as an ivory tower. It has become a battleground between still unrealized utopias and dystopias. Its public moment has to be recovered by expanded access but also accountability. Within the crevices of the capitalist university, there are still spaces of emancipation, teaching being one of the most important. In constituting students as a public, sociology turns itself into its own real utopia.

Part One
Theory and Practice

In contemporary sociology's self-conception, three figures play an especially important foundational or canonical role: Karl Marx (1818–1883), Émile Durkheim (1858–1917), and Max Weber (1864–1920). In the beginning, toward the end of the nineteenth and the beginning of the twentieth century, these three figures were not recognized as founders. The idea of founding figures came much later, after World War II, based on the two dense volumes of *The Structure of Social Action* (1937). They were written by Talcott Parsons, the towering Harvard academic who sought to consolidate sociology around four historic figures – Durkheim, Weber, Marshall, and Pareto. In Parsons' original view they independently converged on a "voluntaristic" theory of social action and a consensual view of society. In his 1949 Presidential address to the American Sociological Association, Parsons (1950) leaves Marshall and Pareto behind to give pride of place to Durkheim and Weber. In the turbulent 1960s, and against Parsons' protests, Karl Marx was added to the pantheon.

Marx was an independent thinker outside the academic world, engaged in politics as well as with political economists and philosophers of the nineteenth century. Durkheim was more centrally placed in the academic world, fighting for a place for the newly created discipline of sociology, especially against psychology. Weber was also deeply involved in university life in Germany and fought for sociology as a new approach to social science from his professorship in political economy.

They each carved out a vision of sociology resting on a set of philosophical assumptions about its object – society or the social. They each proposed a methodology for studying society, often rooted in a broad vision of history, leading to exemplary empirical research that has inspired legions of scholars to follow in their path. But, most important, their theories were rooted in a set of values – freedom, equality, solidarity – that guided what we might call a normative or moral science. Each scientific program wrestles with the question of how those values might be realized – that is the utopian side – and how their realization is obstructed – that is the anti-utopian side. These questions drove a theory of society's permanence and continuity as well as a theory of history, of the future and, thus, of social change. These are the attributes that make Marx, Weber, and Durkheim canonical, necessary attributes for a body of scholarship to enter the pantheon of sociology.

The rare breadth, depth, and vision of canonical figures derive from the battles they fought to have their theories accepted. They had to engage with and borrow from, but also distinguish themselves from, neighboring fields of thought. Once the discipline of sociology was established, those pressures subsided, specialization took off, and the founders could be shed. They were the ladders that got us to the roof; once on the roof, the ladders could be cast aside. But it turns out that the ladders were pillars, too, and without them the roof began to sag. Losing touch with its founders weakens the distinctiveness of sociology as a moral science; it loses sight of itself as a historical actor; it abandons its soul.

If the first chapter of Part One concerns the theoretical foundations of our discipline, the second concerns the practical development of an internal division of labor. As it competed for a place in the academic field, so it advanced as *a professional knowledge* made up of scientific research programs intended for fellow sociologists who together control entry into the discipline. It, therefore, developed its own disciplinary institutions – academic journals, professional association, textbooks, defining problems with paradigmatic research exemplars, university curricula, and examinations. Professional knowledge justified itself not simply as an esoteric knowledge, but also one capable of addressing social problems, what we can call *policy knowledge*, offering its service to clients: corporations, governments, schools, churches. As policy knowledge sold itself to specific clients, so there developed a *public knowledge* that cultivated discussion and debate in the public sphere about the general direction of society and the values that underpin it. Finally, like any other discipline, professional sociology became an arena of contestation. The established research programs come to be challenged by rising generations, who developed *critical knowledge* that calls into question the fundamental assumptions of consecrated professional knowledge. These distinctions, of course, can inform the development of the division of knowledge-practices within any discipline, but here I confine myself to sociology.

Marx, Weber, and Durkheim offer much in the way of guidance and inspiration and their theories have continuing relevance to the problems we face today, but here I want to stress the way they remind us that a flourishing sociology depends upon all four types of knowledge. With specialization, the different knowledges fly apart, lose touch with one another, and the discipline loses its impetus. As professional and policy knowledge come to dominate and even expel critical and public knowledge, sociology suffers a double amnesia. Individually we lose sight of the original motivation to become sociologists and collectively we lose sight of the values that inspired sociology's origins. As the policy moment finds the going tough in a hostile environment, all that remains is professional sociology, which itself then fragments into multiple disconnected research projects. The conceptualization of public sociology seeks to restore the contradictory unity of all four sociologies, recognizing that they sit uneasily together in relations of antagonistic interdependence. Only in this way can we return to the utopian and anti-utopian project that lies at the foundation of our discipline. This is especially important today when the original diagnoses of modernity – anomie, rationalization, alienation, domination, inequality – are coming home to roost, and when utopian thinking is losing credibility. Public sociology inspires the renewal of our discipline.

The entry of W. E. B. Du Bois (1868–1963) into the sociological canon is especially important not only because he centered race in his analysis, not only because he had a global and historical vision, not only because he embarked from lived experience, not only because he was acutely aware of his own place in the world he studied, but also because he uniquely represented all four types of sociology. He circulated restlessly between academic and public worlds, and though he made great contributions to professional knowledge, he never lost sight of the critical sociology that drove it. His research led him to policy advocacy and an array of public interventions that made him unique among sociologists of the twentieth century. He was the greatest public sociologist of the twentieth century. Of all the sociologists, Du Bois was the most sensitive to the antagonistic interdependence among professional, policy, public, and critical sociologies, themselves suspended between utopian imagination and anti-utopian science. He becomes, therefore, the inspiration for a renewal of sociology that is in danger of losing its bearings in the welter of neoliberalism and the centrifugal forces at work within the division of disciplinary labor.

1

Theory

Utopia and Anti-Utopia

As a science sociology is unusual in that it refuses to forget its founders. How is it that we continue to draw inspiration from three European men – Marx, Weber, and Durkheim – from the nineteenth century? From the standpoint of the present they have their inevitable blind spots: a limited focus on questions of race and gender; an often naïve belief in science; and a Eurocentric outlook on the world. They were very much a product of their era and its assumptions.

Indeed, Raewyn Connell (1997) has argued that these so-called classical sociologists had a limited vision of their own times and were arbitrarily chosen after World War II to represent the canon. Upon their shoulders rests the edifice of modern sociology, thereby eclipsing the contributions of a myriad social thinkers from outside Europe. Whereas sister-disciplines like anthropology, economics, and political science have reduced their founders to mere historical interest, Marx, Weber, and Durkheim hang on as obligatory but also inspirational reference points for sociology. Prominent contemporaries, Pierre Bourdieu or Jürgen Habermas, built their social theory on the basis of the same founding figures, implicitly in the case of the first and explicitly in the case of the second. Attempts at building alternative foundations, such as James Coleman's rational choice theory, never made much headway or gained many adherents.

There is, however, one candidate with irrefutable credentials, around whom it is possible to reconstruct the canon – W. E. B. Du Bois. An African American born ten years after Durkheim and four years after Weber, he is of their generation but outlived them by nearly half a century. Educated at Fisk, Harvard, and the University of Berlin, Du Bois pioneered urban sociology at Atlanta University before launching into a public career as a founder of the National Association for the Advancement of Colored People (NAACP), editor of *The Crisis* magazine, and organizer of Pan-Africanism. In 1934 he returned to Atlanta University to complete his extraordinary history of the Civil War and Reconstruction. As he became ever more hostile to the US state that persecuted him, he moved further leftwards, endorsing the socialist vision represented by the Soviet Union and "Communist" China, and ending his life in newly independent Ghana. As a novelist and poet (Du Bois 1911, 1928) he gave sociological theory a uniquely utopian twist that imagined the transcendence of racial and gender domination as well as class exploitation, an optimism always qualified by an anti-utopian science that tragically spelled out the limits of social transformation.

Changing the canon is not simply a matter of adding him to or replacing Marx, Weber, and Durkheim. A canon is always more than the sum of its parts. It refers to a configuration of relations among its members. Du Bois's historically rooted, engaged sociology calls for a reconfiguration of the canon, foregrounding its public and critical dimensions, advancing the duality of utopian imagination and anti-utopian science. I start with the continuing significance of the relations among Marx, Weber, and Durkheim, before pointing to a new canon that incorporates Du Bois's publicly engaged and historically embedded sociology.

The Canon That Was

In whatever ways they may be seen as a product of their times, the founders also rose above their times to speak to the abiding problems of modern society. Marx, Weber, and Durkheim are exemplary not only for their insights into the social world, not only for the methods they used to explore that world, but also for the distinctive way they upheld a science rooted in values. Each managed to establish social constraints – that is, they were anti-utopian, opposing the optimism that anything was possible – but at the same time, they sought to bring the world under human guidance, opposing the pessimistic view that what exists is natural and inevitable. Their sociology was many things, not least a dialogue between its utopian and anti-utopian impulses.

Durkheim's utopia, first spelled out in his 1893 dissertation, *The Division of Labor in Society*, was one in which every individual would find their niche in the division of labor. They would feel at one with the world they inhabited through their mutual interdependence and their contribution to the end product, what he called *organic solidarity*. This would only be possible in a society that offered unimpeded *equality of opportunity* so that everyone has the chance to assume an occupation best suited to their specific talents and abilities. The realization of such a society – a meritocracy – would, however, require radical change: the elimination of unmerited advantages associated with the *"forced" division of labor* in which individuals find themselves in positions for which they are ill-suited. Eliminating the forced division of labor required the end of the inheritance of wealth, but we know today that in addition to economic wealth, cultural wealth (family upbringing, primary socialization) is no less important in determining where in society we end up. To replace the forced division of labor with a meritocracy would require transforming our educational system so as to cancel the abiding effects of social inequalities based on race, class, and gender. Affirmative action aims to counteract such inherited inequalities, while such projects as the Harlem Children's Zone attempt the equalization of opportunities from an early age.

Already a radical project, Durkheim's organic solidarity went even further. Believing that integration into society required not just equality of opportunity, he proposed the elimination of *unjustified inequalities of power*. Workers, he said, would only feel part of the workplace if they were on the same footing as their employer, that is, if they did not fear arbitrary firing, if their boss could not lord it over them. This would call for state regulation of employment relations, as well as state guarantees of minimal existence in the face of unemployment. Employers would have to organize the cooperation of their workers without wielding the threat of dismissal. And if employers were to go out of business, workers and their families would not become destitute but would still obtain a basic standard of living. Thus, today Durkheim might be an advocate of universal basic income – an income unconditionally distributed to all adults that would enable them to subsist. One could envision Durkheim upholding the principles of social democracy that have been approximated in Scandinavian countries. Arguably, Durkheim's vision proposed more than a century ago is both more necessary and more remote today in a world of crushing inequalities of wealth and power and mounting precarity.

Durkheim had a broader vision, a form of guild socialism with the occupational associational as its elemental form. While he advanced the idea of a regulatory state to minimize unjust inequality, he argued that occupational corporations would organize production and inherit property, supplanting the family as the basic unit of society. Durkheim's utopian "normal" division of labor emerged from his anti-utopian analysis of the actually existing "abnormal forms" that impose external constraints on human action. The abnormal forms included not only the forced division of labor rooted in the unjustified and unequal distribution of resources, but also the anomic division of labor in which rapid social change gives rise to states of disorientation (normlessness) and a third abnormal form in which the different parts of society are badly coordinated.

Karl Marx, who never knew Durkheim, would have brought his own anti-utopianism to bear on the idea of organic solidarity and evolutionary progress. He would scoff at the very possibility of realizing such a fantasy under capitalism. The obstacles to organic solidarity, namely, the "external" inequalities of power and wealth, are deeply inscribed in the structure of capitalism: they will not dissolve without a revolution that would overthrow vested interests, especially class interests, in defending capitalism. Durkheim has no way of getting from here to there, from the abnormal to the normal division of labor. Such would be the critique of Karl Marx.

Marx would turn his anti-utopianism against Durkheim's project, but he would also offer an alternative utopia. Thus, Durkheim's guild socialism should not be confused with Marx's communism. Where Durkheim was concerned to *perfect* the division of labor by slotting people into their appropriate places, Marx wanted to *abolish* the division of labor altogether. Slotting people into places crushes their potential to develop rich and varied abilities. They are alienated from their essential being: they don't control what they produce or how they produce it; they don't control the relations through which they produce things. They cannot, in other words, develop their humanity, what Marx and other critical theorists of his time called their "species being."

The barrier to such a world of emancipation is capitalism itself, the incessant pursuit of profit through novel ways of exploiting workers. If they are to survive, capitalists have to compete for profit. They are as trapped by the market as workers who have to sell their capacity to work, their labor power, by the minute, by the hour. His critique of the forces that have hitherto imprisoned humanity led him to conceive of an alternative world of communism that supersedes capitalism – a world free of unnecessary products, from automobiles to nuclear weapons, a world free of unnecessary labor of control and surveillance, a world free of the excessive waste built into capitalism. Freedom from all of these would allow us to reduce the length of the working week, leaving us ample time and space to develop those rich and varied abilities in what he called the "true realm of freedom." As is increasingly recognized, only such a radical transformation of capitalism can avoid the impending human extinction that will come with global warming.

Marx and his lifelong collaborator, Friedrich Engels, clearly saw the virtues of capitalism whose dynamism generated the technology – the forces of production – that made the reduction of the working week possible. Over time, again by its own logic, capitalism destroyed small businesses and concentrated ownership into the hands of large conglomerates and the state, creating the foundations of a planned economy – an economy that would be run and owned collectively, superseding markets and private property. Equally important, capitalism also creates its own gravedigger, in the form of a working class determined to overthrow capitalism and end alienation. The genius of Marx was to discover the laws that bring about the self-destruction of competitive capitalism: competition among capitalists would intensify the exploitation of labor, which would, on the one hand, lead to crises of overproduction and a falling rate of profit, and, on the other hand, assure the organizational ascendancy of the working class. In other words, as economic crises deepened, capitalism enlarged, deskilled, homogenized, and impoverished the working class, forging it into a revolutionary movement that would seize power and turn capitalism into socialism. The utopian and anti-utopian moments finally converge in the miraculous transcendence of capitalism.

Despite their homage to capitalism, Marx and Engels still underestimated its resilience. Their mistake was to believe that the end of competitive capitalism was the end of all capitalism; they failed to anticipate the transition to a new form of capitalism, organized capitalism, orchestrated by a regulatory state that counteracts the crisis tendencies of capitalism – regulating competition, limiting exploitation, and absorbing surplus. Today, there are forces within capitalist society trying to cast off the encumbering state – the very entity that protects capitalism from itself – thereby restoring capitalism's self-destructive tendencies that are as likely to lead to some form of barbarism as communism. Marx's anti-utopian thinking, founded in the atrocities of nineteenth-century textile factories as well as the slavery upon which the cotton industry depended, both of which fed the inexorable expanded reproduction of capitalism, has gained the upper hand as his utopia recedes from the public imagination. Yet we are living in a time when his utopian vision is so desperately needed. As Fredric Jameson (2003: 76) has said, it is easier to imagine the end of the world than the end of capitalism.

We seem, therefore, to be living more in the world conjured up by Max Weber, who mobilized his immense erudition to trace the origins of modern capitalism, precisely because he saw it as an all-conquering expression of a largely irreversible rationalization. Focusing on the obstacles to radical change, he was explicitly skeptical of all utopias, but specifically the Marxist variety. Any attempt at overthrowing capitalism would lead to a horrific world, a dystopia. For Weber the irony of history was the inverse of Marx's optimistic thesis of capitalist self-destruction leading to emancipation. On the contrary, in Weber's *The Protestant Ethic and the Spirit of Capitalism*, for example, individuals start out by acting freely but in the process unintentionally create iron cages for themselves, epitomized by his notion of bureaucracy, the most efficient organization ever invented but also the most indestructible form of domination. Weber was prophetic in anticipating the spread and resilience of institutions bound by rules, discipline, hierarchy, and linear careers. Seeking to overthrow bureaucracy only gives rise to a stronger bureaucracy, endangering liberal-democratic safeguards against its expansion. Socialism, Weber anticipated, would not be the democratic dictatorship of the working class but the authoritarian dictatorship of officials.

Even as he was anti-utopian, Weber, too, harbored a concept of his own utopia – although it was far less radical than the utopias of Durkheim and Marx. According to Weber, it was not possible to perfect the division of labor by securing to each their appropriate place, nor was it possible to abolish the division of labor through transcending capitalism. The best one can do is to treat one's occupation with total devotion. His model was the seventeenth-century Calvinist who considered such devotion to one's occupation as a necessary part of their calling to glorify God on earth. Facing predestination – not knowing whether one was among the damned or the elect – created a deep anxiety, only alleviated by searching for signs of a job well done. In the case of the capitalist, it entailed that most "irrational" of pursuits, accumulation for accumulation's sake, profit for profit's sake, money for money's sake; in the case of the laborer, treating work as an end in itself, instilling the so-called work ethic. Thus, Calvinism gave rise to this spirit of capitalism – that crucial ingredient for the birth of modern capitalism.

The Calvinist is the prototype – or to use Weber's term, the ideal-type – of the modern individual who makes a virtue of necessity through dedication to a life project pursued under uncertain external constraints. Weber makes a similar point in his two famous essays on science and politics, originally addressed to students in 1917 and 1919. Politicians driven by a cause must recognize the radical uncertainty of ever achieving their goal. He describes the inner tension between an ethic of absolute ends involving the single-minded pursuit of a cause irrespective of the consequences and an ethic of responsibility in which the politician takes those consequences into consideration. That's the utopian moment. On the other hand, the politician operates in an institutional context of bureaucracy, party system, and economy that easily subverts the noblest of intentions. "Politics is a strong and slow boring of hard boards" ([1919] 1994: 128).

Weber's limited utopia of "vocation" is the pursuit of a goal whose realization is uncertain, recognizing the anti-utopianism of social constraint – the politician propelled by a mission without guarantees of success. There is a utopian perfection to every occupation – the machine operator, the window cleaner, the domestic worker, the artist, the doctor, the farmer, the manager – whose very unattainability drives commitment. That commitment gives meaning, even to the most mundane activities. As Weber said, it was also true of the scientist. Driven by the puzzles of a research program – puzzles that have meaning only to the cognoscenti – scientists never know whether or when insight will strike. Passionate devotion is a necessary but not a sufficient condition. It is as if breakthroughs lie in the hands of the Calvinist God outside the control of the humble scientist. This devotion to an elusive goal is no less irrational than the pursuit of profit for profit's sake. In both cases any breakthrough, whether new technology or new discovery, is sure to be superseded and forgotten. The only satisfaction is of a job well done, a puzzle solved, a momentary elation, perhaps some honorific recognition. As Weber wrote, not only the intrinsic uncertainty of puzzle-solving but the very institutions of science often favor mediocrity over originality, and are often subject to hostile political regulation. The odds are against us; all we can do is to infuse meaning into our science.

When Weber is at his most bleak after Germany's defeat in World War I, he is driven to assert a utopian moment in uncharacteristically strong terms: "man would not have attained the possible unless time and again he had reached out for the impossible" ([1919] 1994: 128). The darkest days, the most pessimistic times, call out for utopian thinking. When anti-utopia is veering toward dystopia, then the antidote to despair is to remind ourselves how the world has been otherwise in the past and, therefore, how the world could be otherwise in the future.

Reconstructing the Canon

W. E. B. Du Bois would never be satisfied with Weber's bleak prognosis. Making the best of a bad situation was for him a dystopia, personified by his political enemy, Booker T. Washington. Born in 1868 in Great Barrington, Massachusetts, Du Bois grew up in a largely white community and absorbed its Protestant ways. Sponsored by the local community, he went to Fisk University, and from there went to Harvard, where he received a second undergraduate degree and then became the first African American to receive a PhD for his study of the suppression of the slave trade in the US (Du Bois [1896] 2007). He also studied at the University of Berlin, 1892–94, where he witnessed and engaged with the birth of sociology.

Within professional sociology he became known for *The Philadelphia Negro* (1899), a detailed ethnographic study of African Americans in Philadelphia, often seen as the foundation stone of US urban sociology. Although there's no evidence that he had read Durkheim, it reads like an exemplification of the latter's abnormal division of labor, only applied to a racially divided society: on the one side, inequality of opportunity and unequal power, and on the other side a state of anomie resulting from the recent emancipation from slavery and then migration from the South. In *The Souls of Black Folk* (1903: 5), a collection of lyrical essays on the abysmal conditions in the South, Du Bois famously presents the idea of double consciousness: "This sense of always looking at one's self through the eyes of others. ... The history of the American Negro is the history of this strife – this longing to attain self-conscious manhood, to merge his double self into a better and truer self." The striving is to be a "co-worker in the kingdom of culture." The essays are an appeal to the common humanity of Black and white, the forging of a common consciousness through education and religion. The solution to the racial division of labor lies in the cultivation and recognition of African American leaders like himself, the so-called talented tenth. At this point Du Bois has a Durkheimian diagnosis and solution to the racial division of labor, but one without a socialist vision. That is yet to come.

Indeed, as Du Bois became disillusioned by the reception of his ideas, as his work at Atlanta University was largely ignored, as racism became more intractable both in society and in science, as he became more involved in the struggle for racial equality in the Niagara Movement (that prefigured the NAACP that he co-founded), and as he became more influenced by socialist ideas of the time, he became less Durkheimian and more Marxian. In writing the biography of John Brown, leader of an anti-slavery insurrection that prefigured the Civil War, he emphasized a history made from below, so different from his earlier conciliatory politics of assimilation. The mantra of Du Bois's (1909) *John Brown* was: the cost of liberty is less than the price of repression. In other words, the loss of life in fighting slavery is small compared to the atrocities inflicted on slaves.

Darkwater (1920), another collection of remarkable essays, departed from the moral appeals of *The Souls of Black Folk*. Now addressing African Americans, he turns to the souls of white folk and the barbarism they perpetuate in the name of white supremacy, locally and globally. Du Bois now developed a theory of racial capitalism to place the 1917 race riot in East St. Louis in world historical perspective – that was the anti-utopian sociology. At the same time, he advanced a utopian idea of industrial democracy. Moving beyond his early campaign for extending suffrage based on voting qualifications, he advanced a notion of participatory democracy based on the unique and divergent experiences of different groups. Genuine democracy would also require its own economic foundations – freedom from exhausting and demeaning labor. Accordingly, Du Bois proposed the elimination of menial service labor, following the sort of mechanization that had taken place in industry. He wrote of the struggle for women's emancipation led by such heroic African American figures as Harriet Tubman, Sojourner Truth, and Phillis Wheatley, prefiguring the notions of intersectionality that would arrive fifty years later. The reformism of the early years has given way to a radicalism – both in the attention paid to entrenched racial capitalism and in the exploration of alternatives.

In Du Bois's writings utopian and anti-utopian themes reinforced each other in a deepening spiral, reaching a climax in his 1935 masterpiece *Black Reconstruction in America, 1860–1880*. This was a radical rewriting of the history of both the Civil War and the post-war Reconstruction. Famously, he argued that victory for the North was made possible by fugitive slaves joining the Federal army as it was becoming war-weary. Harking back to Marx and his writings on the American Civil War, Du Bois called the desertion from slavery a "general strike," thereby associating slaves with a revolutionary working class. Reconstruction after the Civil War ended when the North abandoned its support for Black emancipation, restoring the power of the Southern planter class that set about imposing new forms of forced labor along with Jim Crow segregation.

But Reconstruction itself was far from the unmitigated disaster painted by historians. In Du Bois's detailed account, the play of political forces harbored possibilities of an inter-racial, radical democracy, albeit varying from state to state depending on historical legacies, racial demographics, and class structure. It was only in the 1960s that historians began to accept the essential truth of Du Bois's redemption of the place of African Americans in

US history. In Du Bois's view, Reconstruction was the last opportunity to transcend race before the consolidation of racial capitalism. As he was writing *Black Reconstruction* during the Depression, Du Bois abandoned the pursuit of immediate integration of African Americans and instead advocated the development of Black autonomy through independent cooperatives, the basis of a cooperative commonwealth. This occasioned another break with the more staid NAACP, which did not waver from a narrow interpretation of "integration."

In the post-war period, as matters looked bleak at home, Du Bois would turn his attention to possibilities abroad. On the one hand, there was his longstanding leadership role in the Pan-African movement that had become ever more real with the major Pan-African Conference of 1945, attended by future leaders of African independence movements. In *The World and Africa* (1947) he developed Marx's idea of the fetishism of commodities, under-lining how invisibly interconnected were the plundering of Africa and the accumulation of wealth in the capitalist West. His global vision took him in another direction – to become an important advocate in the International Peace Movement that was supported by the Soviet Union and opposed by the US state. His defense of the Soviet Union harks back to his first visit in 1926, but his support for "communism" intensified in the post-war period, fueled by the Chinese Revolution. He turned a blind eye to the repressive features of these states, impressed instead by their determined effort to eliminate poverty and reduce inequality.

Although far more radical than Weber, Du Bois, like Weber, recognized that electoral democracy did little to rectify social injustice. Indeed, as he himself experienced, despite its claims to universality, the "democratic" state could deepen injustices. Condemned to be an enemy of the US state, Du Bois confronted its repressive character. For almost a decade he was stripped of his passport, denying him travel abroad. During this period he became closer to members of the Communist Party, actively campaigning for wider civil rights. In the end, he would thumb his nose at the US state, join the Communist Party and leave for newly independent Ghana, where he lived as a citizen for the last three years of his life. He died in 1963 on the eve of the civil rights March on Washington.

How should we place Du Bois in the canon of sociology? In his *The Scholar Denied* (2015) Aldon Morris argues that Du Bois was the true progenitor of urban sociology in the US – his Atlanta School predated and outclassed the so-called Chicago School that had claimed foundational status. Racism excluded him from the major sociology departments and limited his access to resources, yet he was still able to build a thriving school of sociology at Atlanta University, making major contributions to professional sociology. While other African Americans were able to make careers in academia, such as E. Franklin Frazier and Charles S. Johnson, they did so by going along with the dominant tropes that Du Bois rejected. Nor were they so politically active as public figures. Du Bois had a critical disposition that he expressed in public interventions, making him too radical for the social science of the period.

So it would turn out, ironically, that the racism he studied was also the racism that made academia so inhospitable, that drove him into the public sphere, where, for twenty-four years, he became editor of *The Crisis*, one of the great political and cultural magazines of the twentieth century. That gave him a platform for public engagement: whether it was his work documenting and opposing lynching, his key role in the formation of NAACP, his critical engagement with the Harlem Renaissance, his devoted organization of Pan-Africanism, or his opposition to both Booker T. Washington and Marcus Garvey. He was able to speak out in another register with his two novels, *The Quest of the Silver Fleece* (1911) and *Dark Princess* (1928), playing off utopian and anti-utopian themes. From "scholar denied" he became "scholar unbound," lucidly illuminated in his autobiography *Dusk of Dawn* (1940).

Max Weber insisted on a watertight separation of science and politics – the two were governed by opposed logics and confined to divergent arenas. Perhaps Weber's views reflected a period when the university was embattled, when science was still a vulnerable, fledgling pursuit. Although Weber practiced public sociology – including the public lectures he gave at the invitation of students at the University of Munich that were the foundation of his two essays on science and politics – it had no place in his theorization of politics, where he tended to dismiss publics as misguided. The idea of civil society supporting a public sphere was only thinly developed in his work. Du Bois, by contrast, transcended the division between science and politics in both theory and practice. He gave public sociology pride of place in his vision of sociology, not antagonistic to professional, critical, and policy sociologies but as the driving force behind them. This was yet another reason why he was spurned by the professional cadres, and why today his inclusion within the canon redefines the very meaning of sociology.

2

Practice

The (Di)vision of Sociological Labor

If sociology is the prototype of a public science, then South Africa is one of its heartlands. After graduating in 1968 I spent six months in South Africa as a journalist, but I never returned until the lifting of the academic boycott in 1990. In those twenty-two years I continued my interest in South Africa, following the ebbs and flows of apartheid. In 1990 I accepted an invitation to address the conference of the Association for Sociologists in Southern Africa, subsequently reorganized as the South African Sociological Association. I was to make a presentation on the collapse of communism in Eastern Europe, in particular Hungary, where I had been doing research for the previous decade. Given the longstanding association of the African National Congress with the Soviet Union and the rethinking then taking place within the popular South African Communist Party, my talk was of unexpected interest. It was a special time in South African politics – only a few months earlier Mandela had walked out of Robben Island prison, free at last. Especially striking from my point of view was the character of South African sociology – its deep engagement with the struggles against apartheid, and the fascinating developments in industrial sociology, social movements, distinctive feminisms, and studies of violence. This was all on display at the University of Stellenbosch where the conference was held.

How different this was from the US sociology to which I had grown accustomed! I recalled how in 1982 Fernando Henrique Cardoso – then a visiting professor at Berkeley, thirteen years before he would become President of Brazil – was amused by US academics who circulate papers among themselves, publishing articles in professional journals that are typically read by no more than a handful of colleagues. We could be as radical as we wished – and that was a time of the ascendancy of Marxism and feminism within sociology – because outside the university no one was paying any attention. In Brazil, then under military dictatorship, sociologists had to be far more circumspect. There radicalism was a testament to courage and commitment. In South Africa and Brazil, in countries in the Soviet orbit, and, indeed, in many other countries, sociologists were taking their lives into their own hands when they defended critical thinking. Nor did it mean that the content of South African or Brazilian sociology was somehow weaker or less scientific. To the contrary, because so much was at stake sociologists had to do their utmost to get it right. Distinctive theories emerged from their engagement.

After the trip to South Africa in 1990 I returned to Berkeley with a different imagination of what sociology could be, a public sociology very much at odds with my experience of US sociology. When, a few years later, I found myself chair of my department we discussed how we might characterize Berkeley sociology. We agreed that, at least within the US, Berkeley offered a distinctively engaged sociology or *public sociology*.

From Professional Sociology to Public Sociology

Sociology had come late to Berkeley for idiosyncratic reasons. In 1923 the university awarded the irascible Frederick Teggart, autodidact and historian, his own

Department of Social Institutions. It never had more than two full-time faculty but it was an effective buffer against the creation of an independent sociology department. Teggart was openly hostile to sociology, its muckraking disposition and its thin intellectual pedigree. He was not alone. Leaders of the other social sciences on campus also conspired to suppress the discipline. The birth of the sociology department was delayed until Teggart died in 1946. It profited, however, from late development by recruiting up-and-coming sociologists from Harvard, Columbia, and Chicago, and quickly became a leading department in the country.

The 1950s proved to be the golden age for US sociology – the height of Parsonsian structural functionalism that commanded the attention of multiple disciplines, the ascendancy of middle range theory under the inspiration of Robert Merton, the advance of symbolic interaction in Chicago associated with Herbert Blumer and Erving Goffman, the development of survey research and new quantitative techniques that gave new precision to studies of social mobility and stratification, and a precocious comparative history and modernization theory that expanded vistas beyond the US. Berkeley had representatives of all these trends. The next generation, during the 1970s and 1980s, were more radical in their public interventions and more critical of mainstream sociology. They reflected the national agitation for the expansion of civil rights that sparked parallel movements on campus for Free Speech, for Third World representation, and against the Vietnam War. Sociology itself became a battlefield, divided between a complacent professionalism and a turbulent political engagement.

By the time I became chair of the sociology department in 1996, old antagonisms had died down but Berkeley retained a reputation for a more engaged sociology based on the widely read works of its faculty: Bob Blauner, *Racial Oppression in America* (1972); Robert Bellah et al., *Habits of the Heart* (1985); Todd Gitlin, *The Whole World*

Is Watching (1980); Arlie Hochschild, *The Second Shift* (1989); Kristin Luker, *The Politics of Motherhood* (1984); Martín Sánchez-Jankowski, *Islands in the Street* (1991). PhD students were encouraged to turn their dissertations into accessible books as well as articles in professional journals. With Jonathan VanAntwerpen I wrote a history of the department through the lens of public sociology; we held colloquia on public sociology, both its theory and its practice; we even produced an e-book of public sociology contributions from each faculty person. To the consternation of some of my colleagues, students began applying to the PhD program to do "public sociology"!

Public sociology was, after all, a very US concept. In other countries such as South Africa and Brazil, it was taken for granted that sociology had a public dimension. When I would later talk about public sociology abroad, I was often greeted with puzzlement: what else could sociology be if not public? Only in the US did we have to invent a special term to distinguish public sociology from professional sociology – a sociology that is accountable to a community of scientists, a sociology that is largely inaccessible and incomprehensible to lay audiences. In the postwar period, C. Wright Mills best represented the idea of public sociology, both in the monographs he published – *New Men of Power* (1948), *White Collar* (1951), and *The Power Elite* (1956) – and in his critical assessment of mainstream sociology, *The Sociological Imagination* (1959), where he assails the grand theory of Talcott Parsons and the abstracted empiricism of Paul Lazarsfeld. According to Mills, these were the two central tendencies contributing to the degradation of sociology and denying its promise – namely, to stimulate public debate about the big issues of the day.

As I shall be at pains to insist, contrary to Mills, my defense of public sociology in no way implies a rejection of professional sociology. There can be no public sociology without a professional sociology, without the hard-won results of research into inequality, liberal democracy, social mobility, social movements, gender violence, racial orders, education, and so forth. Without professional sociology we would have nothing to broadcast to the wider society except moral critique. A robust public sociology has to be accountable to an equally robust professional sociology. And vice versa: professional sociology needs public sociology or its research programs would ossify, marching to their own tune, ever more detached from the issues of the day. In *The Coming Crisis of Western Sociology* (1970), Alvin Gouldner correctly anticipated that 1950s sociology – proclaiming America to be the paragon of democracy, paradise on earth, and the "end of ideology" – could not survive the escalating demands for civil rights and social justice. But this wasn't to be the end of sociology. To the contrary, the turbulence of civil society in the 1960s infused sociology with new meaning, new paradigms, new categories, new ways of seeing, new utopias to challenge anti-utopian thinking.

From Policy Sociology to Critical Sociology

The engaged sociology of South Africa was one point of reference for what sociology could be; Eastern Europe and the former Soviet Union was another. Throughout the 1980s and 1990s I conducted research, first in socialist Hungary, then in the Soviet Union as it made its transition into a post-socialist world. I will have more to say about that research in subsequent chapters, but in this part of the world sociology was of a very different stripe. Indeed, Soviet sociology foundered on a very rocky road, as it had become a transmission belt for the ideology of the party-state. When a new leadership came to power in the Soviet Union it would set sociologists free to run surveys that would demonstrate popular disaffection with the old regime. As the new leadership consolidated itself, it would force sociology back into a tight corner. In short, Soviet sociology became an instrument of the powerful – what

I call *policy sociology*. It exists in all countries but its most pathological form could be found in Soviet societies where it is presumed that the ruling class – through central planning – represents the interests and needs of the whole population. Today Chinese sociology exhibits similar subordination to the party-state, especially the research conducted in the Academy of Social Sciences that promotes the latest party ideology. In Chinese universities professional sociology is freer, but there too academics are aware of the strict limits on the questions to be asked, and how society can be spoken of.

Still, alongside the policy sociology promoted by authoritarian regimes, there is often an underground *critical sociology* that exposes and opposes the instrumentalization or weaponizing of sociology. In Hungary in the 1970s, there was a flourishing critical sociology. I was especially influenced by Miklós Haraszti's book, translated as *A Worker in a Worker's State* (1977), a riveting account of his experiences working in the Red Star Tractor Factory – despotism at the heart of state socialism. In 1979 George Konrád and Iván Szelényi published their now-classic critique of state socialism, *The Intellectuals on the Road to Class Power*, analyzing the antagonism between a working class of direct producers and an emergent ruling class of intellectuals – "teleological redistributors" who organized and justified the appropriation and redistribution of surplus. In revealing the underlying class character of state socialism, Konrád and Szelényi debunked the dominant ideology of classless society. Szelényi's (1983) urban research in the 1960s demonstrated how market reforms can benefit the working class, just as under capitalism it is the state that benefits the working class. The relative balance of critical and policy sociology under authoritarian regimes varies from country to country and from period to period, accompanying a relatively weak or even nonexistent professional and public sociology. Indeed, if we look across history and across countries we find that the articulation of these four types of sociology is shaped by inherited legacies as well as economic and political contexts.

Defining Four Sociologies

To comprehend the complex relations among the four sociologies, we present them in a matrix motivated by two fundamental questions: Knowledge for Whom? Knowledge for What? In answer to the first question we distinguish between *academic* and *extra-academic audiences*. In answer to the second question we distinguish between *instrumental knowledge* that is focused on the means for a given end, solving puzzles in research programs (professional sociology) or problems defined by clients (policy sociology); and *reflexive knowledge* that is focused on goals, ends, or values, whether it be critical sociology that interrogates the foundations of professional sociology within the academic community, or public sociology that generates public discussion about the overall direction of society. While professional and policy sociologies answer narrowly defined questions, critical and public sociologies uncover the value foundations such questions eclipse.

The tensions among these four types of knowledge are palpable. We have already referred to the relation between professional and public sociology: the former

Table 2.1: The Division of Sociological Labor

		Knowledge for Whom?	
		ACADEMIC AUDIENCE	EXTRA-ACADEMIC AUDIENCE
Knowledge for What?	INSTRUMENTAL KNOWLEDGE	Professional Sociology	Policy Sociology
	REFLEXIVE KNOWLEDGE	Critical Sociology	Public Sociology

Source: Author's own

is theoretical/empirical knowledge that follows scientific norms whose validity is based on correspondence to reality and evaluated by and accountable to peers; the latter is communicative knowledge defined by its relevance to publics whose validity is based on deliberative consensus. I have already argued that the relationship is one of inter-dependence as well as antagonism.

Similarly, policy sociology provides concrete knowledge that serves clients and is evaluated on the basis of effec-tiveness, whereas critical sociology is foundational knowledge with moral vision made valid by normative principles, accountable to a community of critical intel-lectuals. Like professional and public sociology, critical and policy sociology are ostensibly opposed and provide a necessary mutual corrective for each other. Critical sociology reminds policy sociologists of the unspoken assumptions behind their research, just as policy sociology offers an anti-utopian antidote to the utopian proclivities of critical sociology – although policy sociology can also suffer from wishful thinking, as we shall see. Policy sociology, like public sociology, reminds critical sociologists of the relevance of research for the world beyond the academy.

The relationships continue, as professional and critical sociologies are simultaneously interdependent and antago-nistic. Professional sociologists may be annoyed by critical sociologists snapping at their heels, questioning what they take for granted. But professional sociology, nonetheless, requires a critical sociology that interrogates the founda-tional assumptions of research programs – often repressed assumptions that are at the root of the on-going expansion of a given program, assumptions that may also be the obstacle to shifting toward an alternative program, one that is perhaps more consonant with the times. The stronger the professional sociology, the more important the function of critical sociology. In the United States examples of critical sociology are the aforementioned *The Sociological Imagination* by C. Wright Mills and *The Coming Crisis of Western Sociology* by Alvin Gouldner

– both aimed at structural functionalism, both elicited a hostile reaction from consecrated sociologists, both appealed to new generations of sociologists.

A similar antagonistic interdependence governs the relations between public and policy sociology. Policy sociologists, seeking to establish their legitimacy with clients on the basis of their recondite scientific expertise, and operating in private, are threatened by and therefore hostile to the advance of public debate and discussion of the values underlying their proposals. Policies attractive to states with regard to poverty, health insurance, and education may not be so popular with broader publics who have to live with those policies. Anticipated, problematic, or failed attempts at policy formulation often spur public debates that can reverberate back into professional sociology. One has only to think of the debate and research generated by policies focused on crime reduction, school segregation, poverty alleviation, welfare reform, affirmative action, and so much else.

The short-term tension and long-term synergy between instrumental and reflexive knowledge has its parallel in the relation between knowledge geared to academic and extra-academic audiences. Policy sociology can provide the guiding questions and resources for professional sociology, but it can also distort research programs, a tension we find ever more common as universities become strapped for funds. Public sociology can find a greater audience for the discipline but detracts from critical sociology's attention to the discipline's underlying foundations. In brief, the extra-academic pressures can threaten the autonomy of the academic project.

Underlying this scheme is the presumption that all four sociologies are necessary for a vibrant discipline. They form an organic division of labor in which each, potentially, contributes to the flourishing of the whole, but each can also assume a pathological form, threatening the integrity of the whole: when professional sociology becomes self-referential, when policy sociology is captured by clients, when critical sociology becomes dogmatic, and when public sociology devolves into populist appeal or faddishness. In each case the particular type of sociology cuts itself off from the others to the detriment of the discipline as a whole.

Emphasizing the importance of all four types of sociological practice, this scheme courts criticism from all sides because actual sociologists tend to specialize in one or two of these practices, and elevate them to a dominant place in the discipline. Inflating their own importance, representatives of each type of knowledge either assimilate other sociologies under their own umbrella or reduce them to their pathological form, dismissing them as endangering the discipline as a whole. Thus, professional sociologists may claim that they are their own best critics, making a specific critical sociology superfluous, or they may repudiate critical sociology as dogmatic and destructive. Or, most likely, they do both. Again, professional sociologists may claim that going public is part of their day-to-day work or, alternatively, they may dismiss public sociology as pandering to the public. Public sociologists, for their part, may recognize professional sociology as a subordinate wing of their own enterprise or they may dismiss it as self-referential and irrelevant.

So sociology, like any other discipline, becomes a field of struggle. Representatives of a given knowledge-practice assert their control by expelling other knowledge-practices from the field, incorporating them as subordinate partners within the field or by absorbing them into a redefinition of the aggressor's knowledge-practice. The defeated may accept the terms of the dominant or create their own subfield. The resulting unstable equilibrium, reflected in a specific pattern of domination, will vary historically and by country, sensitive to the wider political context.

This matrix can be applied to all disciplines, but each discipline will have its own characteristic pattern of domination: in the natural sciences the instrumental will prevail over the reflexive; in the humanities the reverse might be the case. The social sciences, being in between, can have a particularly unstable pattern of domination between instrumental and reflexive hegemonies.

Competition in the National and Global Arenas

Conventionally, the field of sociology has national parameters so that within each country the four sociologies strike a different balance. But national fields are also embedded in a global field of domination. Northern countries have a monopoly of resources favoring academic autonomy and professionalization, while countries with fewer resources and a more precarious academic order may give more attention to public engagement. Salaries in the Global South may be low, forcing some sociologists into a local-policy sociology or to scramble for consultancies with international organizations. Other sociologists seek ties to the North by writing in dominant languages, primarily English but also French or German, and publishing in Northern (so-called international) journals. The antagonistic interdependence among the different knowledge practices is intensified when the division of labor is projected onto the global arena.

Such global stratification is intensified by global ranking systems based on measures of productivity and recognition. Nation states endorse an evaluation of their universities against the so-called top-ranking universities of the North. Absurd though it may be to have a single set of criteria, evaluating a university in Africa in the same terms as Harvard, such ranking systems are used by states and university administrators to discipline academics and to attract economic investment to their universities or to seek international collaboration. The resulting incentive system has perverse consequences. Orienting oneself to the North – obtaining a degree from the North and aiming to become a global cosmopolitan – usually requires a position in one of the elite Southern national universities. It cuts sociologists off from their less fortunate colleagues, but also from their own communities. Speaking of universities in the Arab East, Sari Hanafi (2011) expressed the dilemmas of the academic: "Publish locally and perish globally or publish globally and perish locally." Competing in the global arena may be so off-putting, so out of their reach, that many turn to local engagement as public sociologists or they simply despair of ever giving their job a sense of vocation.

Thus, inequalities of the global order stamp themselves on the national field. Within northern nations, too, there is an established hierarchy of universities, dependent on the resources they garner, the prestige they hold, the students they attract. And within the university, there is a growing two-tier order separating those who hold tenure-track positions and those employed on a more or less contingent basis to teach. The expansion and differentiation of higher education combines with privatization to increase inequalities at every level. I explore this in more detail in Chapter 15 by expanding the significance of the four types of knowledge-practice.

Sociology's Standpoint: Civil Society

If sociology is a terrain of struggle, what holds it together? What meta-understanding do sociologists share that makes the struggles possible? Here one has to return to the rise of modern sociology. Marx, Durkheim, Weber, and the early Du Bois were writing when sociology was not yet a proven academic field; the division of labor described above was still latent. The dawn of sociology reflected the rise of civil society in Europe and the US at the end of the nineteenth century – civil society understood as the movements, organizations, and institutions that are part of neither the state nor the economy. Civil society represents the drawing of popular classes into a national framework through political parties, trade unions, voluntary associations, social movements that tied family and community to the state. Just as economics took the standpoint of the economy and the expansion of the market, just as political science took the standpoint of the state and the consolidation of political power, so sociology took the standpoint of civil society and the assemblage of collective power.

Sociology reflects the nature of civil society: when civil society disappears, as in Pinochet's Chile or Stalin's Russia, so sociology disappears or goes underground; when civil society is fragmented or precarious, so sociology suffers a parallel tendency. To say that sociology takes the standpoint of civil society is not to say that sociology only studies civil society. To the contrary, it studies politics, economics, and more from the standpoint of civil society. Thus, economic sociology studies the way the market is simultaneously supported by and erodes civil society; political sociology studies the roots of liberal democracy in civil society as well as the way the state consolidates or threatens civil society.

A thriving civil society is a cacophony of institutions, organizations, and movements with roots in a plurality of values – notions of freedom, equality, solidarity – that are at the heart of sociology, motivating its research programs. Civil society, in other words, is the source of a plurality of utopian visions – "real utopias," as Erik Wright (2010) calls them – that sociology uncovers and spreads through discussion and debate in a public sphere. Sociology examines how state and economy depend upon civil society as a condition of their existence, but also how state and economy obstruct – and sometimes facilitate – the realization of the utopian imaginations embedded in civil society. The plurality of values circulating within civil society makes for a plurality of sociologies, a plurality of public sociologies, and a plurality of real utopias. The only value that all sociologists share as sociologists is the commitment to the consolidation and expansion of civil society and an open public discourse that supports it.

Part Two
Policy Sociology

One is not born a sociologist, one becomes a sociologist. As a local lad from Manchester, I don't know what exactly drew me to the United States. But in 1965 at the impressionable age of seventeen, between high school and university, I secured a birth on a Norwegian cargo boat headed for Philadelphia. At that time, from across the Atlantic, the US appeared as a remote colossus; my school friends regarded the trip as, if not treasonous, then deranged. Ostensibly, with my appealing English accent, I was to be employed as a salesman for a New York publishing firm. But that was a nonstarter, since I could not utter a word in such a bewildering city, let alone promote books I knew nothing about. At a loss to know what to do with me, the firm assigned me the absurd task of evaluating the creditworthiness of bookstores across the country.

This was an especially exciting time – the unfolding civil rights movement, anti-Vietnam War teach-ins on campuses, violent protest in ghettos culminating in the Watts Uprising. I had never witnessed such social energy, and, unbeknownst to me, the taste for sociology was germinated. Most immediately, it spelled the end of my interest in mathematics, which had been my passport to university.

After six months in the US, Cambridge seemed parochial and irrelevant. I stuck to mathematics – since I was fit for nothing else and barely fit for that – but took off each summer vacation to explore some other continent. At the end of the first year, 1966, I left for South Africa, a very disturbing place. There I found a more institutionalized, regulated racism than I had known in the US – but then I hadn't spent time in the South. Apartheid affected every arena of life – a repressive order that oppressed all, but obviously some more than others. Below the surface was a seething discontent that would burst into the open in the coming decade – the Durban strikes of 1973, followed by the Soweto insurgency in 1976. After six weeks working in an advertising agency, I took off for three months. With a tent on my back, I thumbed my way through Africa, living off the hospitality of local villagers and townspeople. Episodically, I pursued a little project that began in South Africa – the possibilities of development through correspondence education.

As a young idealist, keen to make the world a better place, I thought if only we understood better and knew more, then we would be sure to progress. Power would wilt in the face of knowledge. What better place to begin, then, with education itself, the organized pursuit of knowledge – its expansion and its dissemination? That is, indeed, where I began, thinking that education could save the world, and if not education itself then its rebellious students. I was after all a child of the times, the turbulent 1960s when anything seemed possible.

I began my initiation into sociology with the exploration of a seemingly esoteric issue, far removed from my own life, the language of instruction in Indian universities. I picked a social problem and tried to solve it – policy sociology as *advocacy*. Sociologists do it all the time, proposing solutions to poverty, inequality, racism. What we discover, however, is that solutions are not easily come by, even less easily implemented, and when implemented are invariably followed by unintended consequences. Such were the anti-utopian lessons I learned in India. Policy sociology is more likely to be where one ends rather than where one begins. So for a more balanced picture I look at William Julius Wilson's (1987) study of the "underclass" and Matthew Desmond's (2016) research on the consequences of eviction. They both aimed to reduce poverty in the US and they both attracted public and political attention.

There is an alternative approach to policy sociology – rather than determining and then tackling the social problem as an autonomous scientist, one can surrender oneself into the captivity of others, solving their problems. It is what I call *sponsored* policy sociology. The solution to a social problem is often already formulated by one's sponsors, so the task is to produce a rationalization and a mode of implementation. We put on their ideological blinkers, turning a blind eye to consequences. I became a servant of power in the employ of multi-national mining companies in Zambia – maintaining the racial status quo while appearing to transform it. The task of the sociologist is to identify with the sponsor and the context they face but to conceal or legitimate assumptions behind the apparent neutrality of expertise. Technical expertise becomes, in the words of James Ferguson (1994), an "antipolitics machine." I will illustrate these processes with an additional example from the sociology of work.

Policy research was too confining, so I did not last long, but I learned so much: first, the importance of the external limits imposed by context on advocacy research; and second, the internal limits set by the (concealed) assumptions of sponsored research. I was well on the way to becoming a sociologist even before I knew it.

3

The Language Question in University Education

Hitchhiking through Africa stimulated an outlandish mission in the summer of my second year at university. I traveled to India to discover whether universities should teach in Hindi, the regional language, or English. Hindi was the national language, spoken by some 30 percent of the population, mainly concentrated in northern India. At that time there were fourteen official regional languages, including ten that were each spoken by more than fifteen million people. English was still a language of the elites, inherited from the erstwhile colonizers who had departed some twenty years earlier. I had hatched this project on a whim after reading a pamphlet put out by the Fabian Society. Being of the view, at that time, that education was the key to development, it seemed like an important question to study.

I had still to learn the limits of the possible whether they concerned my own exploits or the amelioration of the world. This was how I first came in touch with sociology. Although there was no sociology department in Cambridge, there was an American sociologist in residence at King's College every spring. His name was Edward Shils. They said he knew a lot about India, about its intellectuals and about its universities. He was the editor of a journal called *Minerva*, devoted to higher education and science policy. I plucked up courage and knocked on his impressively thick door, that opened into a no-less-impressive chamber. A squat man, avuncular in disposition, beckoned me in and sat me down amid piles of manuscripts. I told him of my plan to travel to India in the long summer vacation and study the problem of the medium of instruction in university education. He looked at me over his glasses to make sure I was not an apparition, then chuckled at my audacity and naïveté. He was amazed that I should have read the tedious reports of Indian Education Commissions – a sign of misplaced seriousness. He gave me a stern lecture on how to comport myself in India and sent me on my way, saying fools march in where angels fear to tread.

No doubt he thought he'd never hear from me again. No doubt I never expected him to dog my career for many years. I had no idea he was one of the most influential sociologists in the US, a close collaborator of Talcott Parsons, or that he was a well-known figure in intellectual circles in England. At that time, I did not know him to be the most learned man that I would ever meet, nor one of the most dangerous. Nor did I have any idea that he was a leading figure in the Congress for Cultural Freedom, a Central Intelligence Agency (CIA) front organization, especially active in Third World countries.

I was not deterred. In those days, access to British universities was the prerogative of a small elite of school leavers. Unless we came from a wealthy background, we were all on some grant or another, whether from local authorities, the state, or the university itself. I was on a state scholarship from which I saved money the previous year for my trip to Africa, and then for my trip to India. My college supplemented my savings with a travel fellowship. With the four-month summer vacation ahead I set out to explore India – a place about which I had read much but had never visited. It would prove to be quite a shock.

I had spent my second year at Cambridge preparing, attending courses in the history of India, reading everything to do with Indian higher education that I could lay my hands on. Accordingly, I all but failed my maths exams, but I left before the results appeared and before anyone could recall me. I had secured a letter of introduction from a professor of education, resident in Cambridge, who had sat on the Indian Commission of Education. The letter was addressed to J. P. Naik, the Undersecretary of the Minister of Education – a revered freedom fighter, humanist, and educator.

I assumed there must be a scientific answer to the question of which language of instruction would be best, so I proposed to conduct a "field experiment," although at the time I did not have the grandiose term to describe what I was doing. I adopted a short and simple essay by Chester Bowles, a famous US ambassador to India, on economic development and taxation policies as the basis of a comprehension test for economics students. I proposed to have the essay and the multiple-choice test translated into Hindi and various regional languages and I would compare how students performed in the different languages.

That was the plan. But it was only J. P. Naik's letter of introduction to Vice-Chancellors of universities in Bombay, Ahmedabad, Chennai, Bhubaneswar, and Lucknow that made this preposterous scheme possible. So that is what I did, traveling third class on trains the length and breadth of India, staying in student dormitories, discussing language issues with anyone who would talk to me. Wherever I went I persuaded some college teacher to translate the Bowles piece into the regional language. I would enter economics classes, randomly divide the students into two groups, and test their comprehension in English as opposed to the regional language. I discovered that in Orissa and Gujarat students performed better in the regional language but in Madras (Tamil Nadu) and, marginally, in Uttar Pradesh (where Hindi is the regional language) they did better in English. A confounding factor was the type of college students attended: whether it was an elite college, like Madras Christian College, where all teaching was conducted in English, or a public state university, as in Ahmedabad, where instruction was already largely carried out in the regional language.

It didn't take long for me to realize the absurdity of the field experiment that took the whole issue out of its social and political context. No field experiment, no matter how sophisticated, could reveal a simple solution. Regional language has the advantage of familiarity, but would there be the resources to develop appropriate terminology, textbooks, journals, teaching materials, and so on? And who will be the teachers in the regional language, potentially cutting themselves off from international developments? If Hindi became the language of instruction, that would have given enormous advantage to the 30 percent Hindi-speaking population, largely in the North. Finally, if English continued to be the medium of instruction, then the low levels of competence among both teachers and students meant that the latter will actually learn very little. At the time I endorsed a compromise solution that seemed to be the best – the creation of "autonomous colleges" where English would be the medium of instruction, but reserving a quarter of the places for students taking exams in the regional language. This would create a bifurcated educational system, differentially resourced, supposedly catering to different talents.

In pursuing the technical function of education – maximizing learning and the dissemination of knowledge – I overlooked the social and political consequences, specifically the reproduction of inequalities. The two-track system might allow for some upward mobility, but it advantaged those with economic and cultural capital, those who came from the professional and upper classes who would have privileged access to the most prestigious education and thus the most prestigious jobs. It was not only a matter of class inequality but also of regional inequality that endowed populations with linguistic capital. What languages one spoke and understood shaped occupational and economic opportunities.

No wonder the language question proved to be such a volatile political issue. The national (trans-regional) elites defended elite colleges, many of them run by Jesuits, inherited from the colonial era, to perpetuate their domination. They did not mind the adoption of regional language as the medium of instruction in provincial universities, so long as they and their children had access to English education, either at home or abroad. They argued that if India wanted to be a modern democracy, integrated into the modern world economy, then Hindi could not replace English as the national language. In this they were supported by elites in the South whose languages were unrelated to Hindi – the possibility that Hindi might be the language of the civil service examinations led to violent protests in the southern state of Madras (Tamil Nadu). If they could not secure the legitimacy of their own regional language, then non-Hindi speakers preferred English. In short, the language question was and has always been far more than an educational issue. It was a political struggle of intersecting class and regional interests, often conducted in the idiom of nationalism.

It was in India that I lost my naïveté, recognizing how technical questions are never simply technical questions, that they are embedded in a wider set of social forces. Even if policies can be manufactured in relative isolation, their implementation will run up against a constellation of shifting interests – in this case the interests of students, parents, teachers, divergent classes as well as real and imagined nations. The language question promoted the centrifugal forces that threatened the unity and viability of India's democracy, but curiously, at the same time, it was through such struggles that compromises were forged, protecting India's unity while reproducing and even deepening social and economic inequalities.

I present this story of my earliest foray into sociology to underline the limits of naïve utopian idealism, but I do not wish to disparage more sophisticated policy advocacy. Let me offer two examples. Matthew Desmond's *Evicted*

(2016) became an instant classic, pointing to the ramifications of housing insecurity for deepening poverty. Based on a participant observation study of low-income white and Black communities in Milwaukee, Desmond explores in captivating detail the causes and consequences of eviction both from the side of the evicted and the side of the landlords. It is a searing exposé of life in the inner city, underlining the necessity of housing security for a minimalist existence. Without a stable home, jobs are difficult to find and retain; without a job rents can be impossible to pay. And yet the policy proposal, like my own in the above case of the language question, fails to address the context within which the housing crisis has developed. Ruling out increasing the supply of public housing, Desmond proposes the expansion of housing vouchers, a market solution that misses the source of housing insecurity in the machinations of developers, real estate, and banks, aided and abetted by municipal government and an abstentionist federal state. When it comes to policy sociology, the danger of participant observation is a misplaced determinism: blaming immediate agents (the exploitative practices of landlords), while projecting a benevolent causality onto unexamined abstractions (expanding markets).

The distinguished and influential sociologist William Julius Wilson – who would also be my supervisor at the University of Chicago, and we'll get to that later – would not pin his hope on the market but on the state. His career shows both the limitations and the possibilities of policy sociology and how closely it has to be connected to public, critical, and professional sociology. Wilson lit a fire of controversy with his second book, *The Declining Significance of Race* (1978). Here was an African American scholar at the University of Chicago, seemingly trumpeting a very conservative thesis. His book might as well have been titled "the increasing significance of class," but that would not have stimulated the ferocious debate that followed its publication. Wilson traces three

successive racial orders, starting with slavery and ending
with the postwar period, which he characterizes as class
polarization within the African American community.
The civil rights movement, dominated by middle-class
Blacks fighting for inclusion through such policies as
affirmative action, largely overlooked the impoverishment
of an increasingly marginalized and destitute population
of African Americans. He is not denying racial discrimi-
nation but insists class increasingly determines the life
chances of African Americans.

Defending his claims against African American critics
and repudiating the embrace of neo-conservatives, Wilson's
next book, *The Truly Disadvantaged* (1987), advanced
a research program directed at what he provocatively
called the "underclass," a term used by conservatives to
blame the poor for their own poverty, handicapped by an
inherited "culture of poverty." Liberal sociologists and
African American critical race theorists, being allergic to
victim blaming, were aghast at Wilson's willingness to give
credence to the pathologies of the ghetto – criminality,
drug abuse, female-headed households, gang warfare, and
so on. While recognizing cultural factors, Wilson argued
that structural factors also played a role in the persistence
of poverty, such as the exodus of middle-class Blacks and
the disappearance of working-class jobs, which emptied
the ghetto of its means of survival. His research program
expanded into what became known as the neighborhood
effects literature – how neighborhood characteristics affect
poverty. In his next book, *When Work Disappears* (1996),
his policy proposals became clear – job creation through
an active labor market policy. It was not that African
Americans had developed a dependency on the state and
thus a disinclination to work. It was not an absent work
ethic that explained their destitution. It was simply a
shortage of decent jobs.

This was the period of President Clinton's welfare
reform. Wilson's ideas were twisted into support for
workfare – welfare tied to work, to the search for work,

or to job training. Wilson insisted on the contrary: forcing people into lousy, precarious, poorly paid jobs was no answer to poverty. He lost the policy battle but he did ignite a public debate about the sources of poverty. He understood that if he was to be successful as a policy sociologist it was necessary to drum up public pressure behind his proposals. His sensitivity to the multiple interests in the political field led him to advocate universal as well as targeted policies, but he was under no illusion as to the uphill battle he faced in a period of neoliberalism. If the political winds were blowing against his proposals then not even all his fame, distinction, influence, and research could move the state.

4

Job Evaluation in a Racial Order

I returned to Cambridge and wrote up my findings on the language question in Indian universities. I knocked on Professor Shils's door once again, this time to hand him my report. Remembering my first visit, he looked at me, incredulous. To his credit he said he would read it and told me to return the following week. That year I became a regular visitor to his chambers in King's College as I became a specimen of the "reviled" student rebellion overtaking universities. He offered to have my report published in his journal, *Minerva*, presumably after he had rewritten it to his liking. I declined the offer, fearing what would become of it. In his benevolent way he told me I needed to cut out my wild schemes and get down to a serious training in sociology, which, he assured me, could only be obtained in the US. But I had other plans.

For now I had to get this degree in mathematics – quite a challenge given how much time I had devoted to my Indian escapade. Somehow I survived the ordeal but that was the end of my interest in being a student. Instead, after graduating in 1968, I immediately returned to South Africa where my color gave me access to a journalist job that would be quite beyond my reach elsewhere. I joined the staff of *News Check*, a newly created weekly magazine, styled after the US magazine *Businessweek*, whose editor, Otto Krause, was a rising star in the liberal wing of Afrikaner politics. I was assigned to the section on foreign affairs – the back pages of a magazine that mainly focused on South Africa. Writing to deadline on topics about which I knew next to nothing was discipline indeed. Still, 1968 was an exciting time to be reporting on foreign news – the year of great student movements not just in Europe and the US but across the globe, the year of the ugly Biafra–Nigeria Civil War, the year of the Prague Spring. In South Africa things were bleak, yet for those in the know, there was a stirring in the belly of the beast, most notably the Black Consciousness Movement. Social transformation was in the air, all over the world.

After six months of journalism in South Africa, I retraced my previous hitchhiking path northwards to Zambia – the path I had taken two years before. It was now four years after the country had won independence in 1964. Although I was in pursuit of sociology and student movements, I also needed to earn a living. I knocked on the door of Jack Simons – South African communist and anti-apartheid fighter, living in Lusaka in exile. Apart from his political engagement, he had been a distinguished anthropologist and political scientist, teaching at the University of Cape Town. He was now teaching in the sociology department at the new University of Zambia.

We know a lot about the conditions of the miners, Simons told me, but we know so little about the mining companies and their dealings with the new Zambian government. So I followed his suggestion and looked for a job with Anglo American, one of the two multinational corporations that owned and ran the lucrative copper mines. I contacted a senior executive who had put me up on my previous trip through Zambia. I was in luck: copper prices were high and "qualified" expatriate labor was in demand. I landed a position in the copper industry's Personnel Research Unit. As it turned out, I couldn't have been better placed to understand the responses of the mining companies to Zambian independence.

The Personnel Research Unit (PRU) had been recently created as a research wing of the Copper Industry Service Bureau, located in Kitwe at the heart of the Copperbelt. I was given free rein to study such things as patterns of absenteeism, labor turnover, work stoppages, disciplinary measures – which, I discovered, were being misused by Zambian political leaders to excoriate mine workers as slothful and unpatriotic. Later I would re-examine these same figures to criticize the claims of a then young political scientist, Robert Bates (1971), who was echoing the government's view that, with independence, workers were not pulling their weight in their contributions to nation building (Burawoy 1972b).

One of the core tasks of the PRU was to service the job evaluation scheme that had evolved to justify the pay scales of the mining industry's approximately 50,000 African and expatriate employees. Each job was evaluated on the basis of a list of factors, such as skill, training, education, effort, and responsibility, so as to produce an appropriate and consistent payment system. The scheme had developed as a way of rationalizing African advancement in the colonial period when, under pressure from African unions, expatriate (white) jobs were slowly fragmented and passed over to Africans. Expatriates with long experience in different parts of the mining industry maintained the system, responding to grievances and changes in job descriptions. In this regard the colonial context had produced a rather effective machinery of modern management, but there was a snag. There had always been two job evaluation schemes, corresponding to two pay scales and two different job ladders, one for Blacks and one for whites. Four years after independence this was now unaccep-table – if it meant anything, postcolonialism meant the end of the colonial racial order. The union was demanding a single wage structure, and they wanted to participate in its construction. This could no longer be controlled by a clique of expatriate old-timers.

But how to integrate these two wage structures, especially as most of the expatriate jobs were qualitatively different from the jobs held by Zambians? Could one even devise a single job evaluation scheme to embrace such disparate job structures? Equally important, the integrated wage structure could not disturb the existing job hierarchies within and between races. They brought in consultants from the UK whose experience with job evaluation was limited to a small Kleeneze factory in Birmingham. Dealing with the copper industry of 50,000 employees and several thousand different jobs, they were quickly out of their depth. I was a silent observer in these matters, as I too had no expertise in the jobs of the mining industry. Still, it did occur to me that this was an intriguing mathematical problem of optimization under constraints. Management became so desperate that they were willing to give me the chance to rescue the situation.

Any job evaluation system rests on the prior determination of a ranking of a given set of carefully chosen key jobs. In this case there were twenty key jobs representative of the industry as a whole. They each had to be allotted points based on the evaluation of each of the factors – each factor having a series of levels. The trick was to determine a *weighting* of each factor so as to arrive at the correct, predetermined ranking of the key jobs – a ranking that reflected the existing hierarchy. To establish the factor weightings that would assure the correct ranking was a linear programming problem that any computer could solve. There was a lot of trial and error in determining the key jobs, both which ones as well as how many, and deciding on the factors, both what factors and how many levels within each. We experimented with broader batches of jobs until we arrived iteratively at a final scheme of factor-levels and factor-weights that fitted the constraints – maintain the old hierarchy of jobs within a new integrated system – whereupon management and union representatives could set about evaluating all the jobs in the industry. The inclusion of union representatives on the job evaluation team was new, but they were not involved in creating the underlying system that was designed to reproduce the old racial hierarchy of jobs. Their participation in the laborious work of evaluation legitimated the new system but the results were preordained by the original ranking of key jobs.

Well, this is how I now interpret what I was doing then. At the time it was simply a mathematical puzzle. I didn't know what I was doing sociologically: I was absorbed in the technicalities and blind to the wider implications. The application of a standardized rubric to all jobs concealed an arbitrary judgment – a systems of factors, weights, and levels designed to give a specified ranking of key jobs that would translate into an unchanged hierarchy of all the jobs in the mining industry! Assumptions in, assumptions out. As a technician it was so obvious to me that it did not even bear reflecting upon. But as a budding sociologist it did warrant reflection – it was a technique to produce the appearance of race neutrality by integrating Black and white wage scales in a way that didn't threaten the status quo, and that favored the skills and experience of white workers. Today we'd call it the production of color-blind racism.

Absorbed by the challenge of making it work, I became a policy sociologist employed to resolve a problem defined by the mining companies, as they engaged in delicate negotiations with the trade unions. I was there to accomplish the integration of the wage structures without generating political repercussions that might have destabilized the industry, making it all appear as the magical product of scientific rationality. The foundation of the whole system was obscured from public vision. In Max Weber's terms I was advancing formal equality to hide and reproduce substantive inequality. I was not myself deciding the policy issue, but it was decided for me. My task was to rationalize a decision that had already been made. I had become a servant of power.

There was a lot at stake. As a legacy of colonialism and its singular focus on extraction of raw materials, the copper industry supplied 95 percent of Zambia's foreign revenue. It was a sacred cow. Four years after independence neither government nor trade unions could countenance the overt continuity of a racial order but neither could they risk undermining the racial hierarchy, for fear this would lead to intensified conflict and even the exodus of badly needed expatriate expertise. The production of an integrated wage structure based on job evaluation was the perfect solution, once it was made technically feasible.

In the study of the language problem in Indian higher education my crude field experiment *blotted out* the political context, making the results largely irrelevant; by contrast, in developing the job evaluation scheme for the Zambian mines the political context was *built into* the underlying assumptions of its design. Policy research often combines advocacy that overlooks context and sponsorship that takes conditions for granted. Thus, pioneering research that established a sub-discipline in the sociology of work was conducted at Western Electric's Hawthorne Plant in Chicago from 1924 to 1933 (Roethlisberger and Dickson 1939). A team of social scientists led by Elton Mayo of the Harvard Business School investigated the effects on productivity of changes in lighting, breaks, length of the working day, and the payment system. Unable to tie productivity directly to changes in the environment, they instead identified a pattern that linked increases in output to the experiments themselves. The researchers claimed that by being the subjects of an experiment and, thus, awarded attention, workers increased their productivity. This became known as the Hawthorne effect, and became the basis of the human relations school of management: Pay attention to your workers and they will work harder.

The story does not end there. Re-examination of the original qualitative data by Alex Carey (1967) and the original quantitative data by Richard Franke and James Kaul (1978) called into question the "Hawthorne effect"

– 90 percent of the variance could be attributed to three factors: managerial discipline, fatigue, and economic adversity due to the Depression. The managerial biases behind the Hawthorne Experiment and Elton Mayo's own disposition to look for "human factors" led to an erroneous theory of worker motivation. The revisit showed how the Hawthorne researchers missed the context in which the experiment took place, namely, deepening economic crisis and increasing unemployment that lay behind management's ability to extract greater effort from workers.

The Western Electric studies remain a classic case of policy sociology, conducted at the behest of management. They generated a research program in industrial sociology that highlighted the social dimensions of work; they also inspired a critical sociology that attacked industrial sociology as managerial ideology, an indictment that some would extend to policy sociology more broadly.

While working at the PRU I was only dimly aware of the problematic Western Electric studies. However, I did not need to know about them to develop misgivings about my research as an employee of Anglo. For I was developing another agenda, a secret agenda. Following Jack Simons's suggestion, I was burrowing from within to understand how corporate decisions were made. As the mining companies were deploying my mathematical skills, they were giving me unique insights into high-level negotiations with the trade unions, as well as access to all sorts of company documents. I even milked the companies for resources to run a social survey of miners, what I then believed to be the special technique of sociological research. The mining companies were very pleased with my work. As a servant of power they rewarded me with a scholarship to go to the University of Zambia, where I got my first degree in sociology (combined with anthropology).

The mining companies may have been happy with me, but I was not happy with them. As I became a student of sociology, I reflected upon my experience in management. I was appalled by their complicity in supporting the racial hierarchy in the industry, what was known as the *color bar* – a quintessential expression of colonialism that was supposed to have dissolved. I realized how I too was complicit in its persistence, leading me to wonder what explained this reproduction of racism. I began to study the very process to which I had contributed.

Part Three
Public Sociology

It was naïve to think that sociology could present simple solutions to complex problems. The first lesson in sociology was to recognize that "social problems" cannot be divorced from the *context* out of which they arise and within which they swim. In the academic cloisters of Cambridge I could be narrowly focused on the question of the medium of instruction as though it were separate from the wider society, but once I arrived in India it was impossible to ignore the politics and social movements swirling around the language question.

It was no less naïve to think that powerful actors would use sociology for the benefit of all. The second lesson, therefore, was that behind any solution to a social problem were a set of *interests*. To be sure the mining companies were compelled for political reasons to introduce an integrated wage structure, but the solution they developed (with my help!) was to preserve the existing organization and racial hierarchy. In short, following the French sociologist Pierre Bourdieu, one can think of the context as a field of actors with competing and conflicting interests.

My forays into the world of policy making exposed the social constraints on the feasible: both the constraints of context made up of actors and institutions and the constraints of interests carried by actors and embedded in institutions. Public sociology turns public attention onto those constraints. It carries sociology into the public realm for an open dialogue, precisely on the limits of the possible and how those limits could then be transcended – the anti-utopian and utopian visions. As the next two chapters show, such public initiatives are also fraught with dilemmas and challenges, pointing to the third lesson of sociology – that the actors in a political field not only have different interests, but they also have a different capacity to realize those interests, what we call *power.*

In the first case of public sociology I attempt to expose racial practices in postcolonial Zambia not as a function of individual prejudices but as a function of class interests. By pointing to the strength of class interests inherited from the colonial order I underline the obstacles to social change in the hope that public awareness might lead to their mitigation or diversion. In propagating such an analysis one always has to be aware of the constellation of powers within the public realm. A sociological message critical of the mining industry, of the state, of the new ruling class can be suppressed or even mobilized in defense of the dominant powers.

Transmitting sociology via media into the public realm, what I call *traditional public sociology*, has to face the power asymmetries of that mediated world. It is often most effective when it does not directly challenge dominant powers, or launches itself in moments of crisis when the dominant are themselves divided or otherwise losing their power – their hegemony – over the dominated. In the case study below the mining companies were able to deploy my critical class analysis of their operations for their own ends.

An alternative approach to public sociology, what I call *organic public sociology*, is to avoid the distortions and interests of the media and instead pursue an unmediated engagement with publics. It means that the sociologist has a face-to-face relation with a more limited public, but one that is better organized and more determined. This was the case of my study of student rebellion. I was a student at the University of Zambia; I lived on campus alongside other students; I was arrested with them. In other words, I participated in their projects, trying to understand their contribution to social change. I was accountable to them and when I steered my own course they rejected me. Organic public sociology has its own dilemmas to be negotiated – the dilemma of autonomy in collaboration.

5

The Color of Class

I had arrived in Africa at an exciting moment. During the late 1950s and the 1960s, nation after nation secured its independence from colonial rule. Africa was no longer governed from London, Paris, or Lisbon, but would govern itself, bringing political if not economic equality to all citizens, allowing them to vote in their own elections, giving them access to education, living where their means allowed rather than where their race determined. By 1968, when I arrived in Zambia, colonial orders had dissolved all over the continent except in its southern cone. At that time South Africa, Southern Rhodesia (now Zimbabwe), Angola, and Mozambique were the last redoubts of settler colonialism.

Zambia, previously Northern Rhodesia, had won independence in 1964, and four years later the shine was still on; the country was breathing optimism, President Kaunda was preaching Zambian Humanism, a variant of African Socialism. Social scientists debated development and democracy, socialism and revolution. There was an air of hope that Africa would point the way forward beyond the Cold War, escaping the traps of Western capitalism and Soviet communism. This was a utopian moment if ever there was one, but anti-utopian clouds were gathering on the horizon: "dependency," "neocolonialism," "tribalism," and dictatorship.

Frantz Fanon, prophet of the African Revolution and author of *The Wretched of the Earth* (1961), best captures the dialectic of utopian and anti-utopian thinking. Fanon distinguished two trajectories out of colonialism: the National Bourgeois Road that ends with a dependent dictatorship and the National Liberation Struggle that ends with democratic socialism. The former involves the replacement of white by Black, of a colonial administration by an African government, essentially a recoloring of the existing class structure. This was the capitalist road supported by an aspirant Black bourgeoisie largely composed of civil servants, teachers, lawyers, doctors, nurses but also a labor aristocracy of wage laborers whose position was more secure than the dispossessed peasantry. Fanon regarded the capitalist road as ruinous. But this was less to do with the attributes of the African successors, and far more to do with the peripheral or dependent capitalism that was Africa's unavoidable fate. Unlike in the West, capitalism in Africa could not support a liberal democracy, could not provide the material basis for redistributive concessions that are democracy's lifeblood. He predicted that any experiment in multiparty democracy would degenerate into a one-party state and then to a one-man dictatorship.

The National Liberation Struggle, on the other hand, would overthrow the existing class structure and introduce a democratic socialism based on the full participation of its people. The driving force behind such a revolutionary regime would come from the dispossessed peasantry led by dissident intellectuals fleeing the towns. The two movements – National Bourgeois Road and National Liberation Struggle – would struggle for hegemony over the remaining classes – tribal chiefs and the urban lumpenproletariat – thereby determining the trajectory of the postcolony. If the National Liberation movement's socialist goal proved to be an elusive utopia, Fanon's anti-utopian anticipation of the capitalist road proved to be tragically prophetic. Nonetheless the two visions, the utopian and the anti-utopian, fed off each other, defining each other and illuminating the stark reality of Africa.

Fanon's powerful vision was nonetheless limited by his experiences in Algeria, of settler colonialism rooted in agriculture. Zambia inherited a very different class structure, calling for a modification of Fanon's theory. Northern Rhodesia was administered to expedite the extraction of its copper deposits. Agriculture involved a partial dispossession and taxation of the peasantry to create a cheap migrant labor force on the one hand, and food to feed the urban working class on the other. In Zambia, there was no sign of a revolutionary peasantry nor of an independence struggle that would turn into a civil war. There was a smooth transfer of power as the nation eased into the National Bourgeois Road, proclaimed to be Humanism, President Kaunda's version of African Socialism.

The copper industry, as the engine of economic development, and not settler agriculture, became the focus of postcolonial reconstruction. It generated its own politics revolving around mine ownership, the improvement of the conditions of the miners, and who would be managing operations. In particular, how would the racial order in the mines be reorganized? As I have narrated in the previous chapter, historically, the color bar had ruled the industry – so what happens to the color bar in postcolonial Zambia? How does the replacement of white by Black, the rise of an African bourgeoisie, affect the racial order?

When I arrived in Lusaka in 1968, the government had just issued a report on "Zambianization" in the copper mines – the localization of the labor force that involves racial succession. It was a congratulatory report that documented a great success. Below I reproduce the table from that report, capturing the progress made since independence. Sure enough, the number of Zambians in managerial positions had increased five-fold. At the same time the number of expatriates had fallen. Undoubtedly, this was a success story, but was it only a success story?

The report fails to mention that the number of expatriates displaced (2,597) is less than the number of Zambians promoted (2,967), which suggests an inflation of the supervisory and managerial ranks. Why might this be the case? To answer that question would require me to study the micro-processes that lay behind these macro figures.

The job evaluation exercise suggested there might still be a racial hierarchy in terms of pay scales, based on a specific set of attributes of jobs, but it didn't tell me what happened to the structure of positions. What had happened to the colonial color bar according to which no white should ever be subordinated to a Black person? This would require an examination of the process of racial succession. How would this be possible? I certainly couldn't openly declare I was studying Zambianization, as that was far too politically sensitive. Had management known what I was about I would have been chased off the mines and that would have been the end of the research.

I had, therefore, to undertake *covert* research, but of a particular sort, research conducted in the time and space of the subjects themselves. Sociologists call this *participant observation* when observation takes priority over participation or *observant participation* when participation dominates observation (Seim, forthcoming). It was important to watch the process of racial succession as

Table 5.1: The Progress of Zambianization

	Total No. of expatriates	Total No. of Zambians in the field of expatriate employment
December 1964	7,621	704
March 1966	6,592	1,138
September 1966	6,358	1,884
October 1967	5,671	2,617
June 1968	5,024	3,671

Source: Government of the Republic of Zambia (1968: 9)

it unfolded over time in particular workplaces. To that end I enrolled the help of students from the University of Zambia to work in the mines and follow these processes – a form of observant participation. They were paid by the mining companies to do research on working conditions. We made no mention of Zambianization to management, although we discussed it at great length among ourselves.

Accordingly, as well as collecting data from informal conversations, we undertook a series of case studies of Zambianization – observing what happens when a Zambian replaced a white expatriate employee. Take the position of mine captain – which was the highest level of management working underground, and was just beginning to be Zambianized when we arrived. What happened when a Black shift boss (the next level down in the managerial hierarchy) was promoted to replace the white mine captain? It was as simple as it was shocking: the white mine captain was displaced upwards but not removed. He was promoted into a newly created position on surface – assistant to the manager of underground operations.

This effectively protected the color bar, but at the cost of creating tensions throughout the organization. The new assistant underground manager took with him many of the resources and much of the influence that he previously possessed as a mine captain. This left the Black mine captain with the same responsibilities as his predecessor but not the organizational support to carry them out. The immediate subordinate of the now Black mine captain – the Black shift boss – found his job more difficult because his supervisor was organizationally so much weaker. He came to resent his new Black supervisor, even to the point of wishing for the return of the previous white mine captain. Tensions reverberated all the way down the hierarchy, inspiring hostility to Zambian successors who came to be seen as an uppity class, in thrall to white management. The Zambian successor, himself, led a very insecure existence, criticized from every side as incompetent, thereby feeding racial stereotypes and making his life even more difficult. He might seek to alleviate his anxiety by pursuing an ostentatious lifestyle, which only intensified class hostility from fellow Zambians.

The lived experience in the mines led workers and managers alike to discredit Black successors, blamed for incompetence, while the underlying reality driving this lived experience lay with the strategies to reproduce the color bar. This raises the bigger question: if independence meant the end of racism, why did the color bar persist? How and why does colonialism continue to unfold within postcolonialism? In particular, why should the color bar continue in the Copperbelt when it was being dissolved in government, where Zambianization proceeded from the top down as well as the bottom up? If the first sociological move was to examine the lived experience in the mines, the second move was to link those micro-processes to macro-forces, extending beyond the everyday common sense of participants to the wider political and economic influences at work.

Guided by the Fanonite framework I had adopted, I teased out the interests tied to different positions in the class structure of the postcolony. The Zambian working class – the skilled and semi-skilled miners – laboring in the most dangerous conditions, were not interested in Zambianization, the creation of a new class of overlords, but in improving their own wages and working conditions. White managers – and management was still largely white – were even less interested in removing the color bar, since they wanted to hold on to their lucrative jobs – their skills were often specific to the Zambian mines and not easily deployed in other workplaces. They also wanted to protect their racial enclave, both at work and in the community. Corporate management, on the other hand, found itself in a quandary: on the one hand, it was interested in promoting Zambianization and dismantling the color bar as this would lower labor costs; on the other hand, they did not want to upset the apple cart by alienating white managers who were not easily replaced, given the special skills they had acquired.

As I discovered – and it was a real discovery – when working in the PRU, corporate management did not have a fixed strategy or plan, but would wake up each morning and assess the direction of the winds. Finding themselves in an uncertain political environment (government and labor relations), economic environment (price of copper), and technological environment (unexpected challenges of exploration and development), which they did not control, corporate management adopted a flexible decision-making process. It let the government take the lead on the matter of Zambianization, which was especially convenient because the government turned a blind eye to the color bar – or so it seemed – for fear of jeopardizing the foreign revenue generated by copper exports. Moreover, from the standpoint of the party-controlled government, having expatriates running the mines was preferable to Zambians, who might form an effective political opposition. Expatriates on three-year contracts could be removed if, in the unlikely event, they ever presented any such threat. In addition, given the colonial legacy, there was a real constraint – a shortage of qualified Zambians to take over the running of the mines. In short, with the exception of the Zambian successors themselves, none of these "class" groupings had an interest in removing the color bar and demolishing the inherited colonial racial order. In moving from micro-processes to their macro-foundations, I was able to identify the class interests behind the postcolonial racial order.

Having undertaken this analysis, unbeknownst to the mining companies but based on company data, informal interviews, and three years of detailed observations of successions, I had to decide whether to turn this organizational pathology into a "public issue" and, if so, how. As an unauthorized exposé, my report could spell the end of social science research on the mines, I realized. So I made an appointment with Anglo American executives in

Lusaka – the ones who had sponsored my research. My report was received with shock and dismay, and a blank refusal to allow publication. But, I pleaded, "It's based on your data." That may be, they said, but we don't agree with your interpretations, especially that management deliberately upholds the color bar. Faced with my insistence that this was too important to be pushed under the carpet, and perhaps fearing I might leak it to the press anyhow, they sent me to the Ministry responsible for the copper mines, on the grounds that the mines had recently been nationalized. My attack on the government was even more scathing than my criticism of the companies, so we both knew that this was a clever deflection of responsibility.

But we were both wrong! The person responsible for Zambianization in the Ministry, ironically an expatriate with experience in the mines, read my report with enthusiasm and instructed me to get it published as quickly as possible. I was astonished. Apart from anything else, his action refuted my claim that the state was a monolithic entity intent upon preserving the color bar – there were clearly differences within the state and I would have to revise my theory.

The report was duly published as a monograph by the Institute of African Studies at the University of Zambia – what had been the Rhodes-Livingstone Institute, a leading center for colonial-era anthropological studies. When *The Colour of Class on the Copper Mines* appeared in 1972, it received much publicity in newspapers and on television. The discussion did not turn into recrimination against expatriates or government or mining companies; there was a real sense of social constraint, forces beyond the control of individuals. As is usually the case with public debate, it is difficult to assess its influence, but what was important was the opening up of discussion; the silence had been broken.

Most curious was the response of the mining companies. Rather than emitting a battery of denials, they used this Marxist-Fanonian report to discipline their own mine

management, requiring them to get their Zambianization
house in order. Public sociology led to internal interventions and became, you might say, policy sociology. But
these interventions were limited; the color bar floated
upwards perhaps, but the color bar remained.

Once again I had to face my own political naïveté. I was
so appalled by this blatant reproduction of racism that I
thought if only it were widely known, the force of public
opinion would compel reform. I had still to learn that
knowledge does not have its own impetus, truth does not
have its own power, it can be mobilized and distorted by
powerful actors for their own ends. The public sphere is an
uneven playing field in which unequally endowed actors
compete to have their interests prevail. If class analysis
applied to the process of racial succession, it also applied
to the dissemination of research, first whether it is ever
heard at all, and on those rare occasions that it is heard,
the struggle over its interpretation and use.

6

Student Rebellion

The Colour of Class on the Copper Mines (1972a) represented *traditional* public sociology, transmitting sociology to wider audiences in the hope of generating public debate. It aims at a form of public education: developing a sociological appreciation of the way everyday experience is subject to internal as well as external constraints, and thus opening the possibility that things could be otherwise. Here sociology competes with messages from neighboring disciplines but, even more significantly, with official and unofficial media, and today social media, that have a grip on the terms of public discussion, a grip that panders to common sense, often at odds with sociology. Traditional public sociology can be an uphill battle.

There is, however, an alternative type of public sociology – *organic* public sociology – in which the sociologist has direct access to publics, in which the sociologist and public enter into an *unmediated* face-to-face relation. Instead of a broad, thin, passive, and mainstream public, organic public sociology encounters or creates narrow, thick, active counter-publics. If traditional public sociology's reliance on media entails losing control of the message, the more confined engagement of organic public sociology restores a semblance of control but at the cost of wider visibility. In this next project I engaged directly with the students at the new University of Zambia (UNZA). They, too, were a successor generation – largely, to a Zambian ruling class – and as an aspirant class developed a hostile relation to those they would replace.

After working on the Copperbelt for a year and a half, I registered for an MA in sociology and anthropology at the University of Zambia. There were just two of us – an African student from Zimbabwe and myself. The degree was beset with controversy from the beginning. How could an under-resourced university in the Third World justify devoting so much time to training two students, neither of whom were Zambians nor had a background in sociology? Still, the chair of the department, Jaap van Velsen, insisted that it would be good for the department to have an MA program and this would be a good way to begin.

It was painful for both of us. We were thrown in at the deep end and we just had to learn to swim. The three senior faculty – an overpowering Dutchman trained as an anthropologist, a South African freedom fighter and learned academic, and a young anthropologist from Delhi – competed with one another to destroy our weekly essays. All three were broadly Marxist in orientation and that is how I, too, became a Marxist. In hindsight I was the fortunate recipient of a terrifying force-fed education in sociology and anthropology. I've never learned so much so quickly and under such duress.

Those were heady days when one felt, as a social scientist, that one was at the center of a turbulent trans-formation of society, in which utopian and anti-utopian visions openly clashed. What one was learning, even the most romantic anthropology, had immediate relevance to the challenges of national reconstruction. The multidisci-plinary seminars held in the school of social science had an air of excitement – which I have rarely experienced again – as our research was connected to Zambia's exit from colonialism and entry into a new world. Debates that opposed socialism to capitalism had a sense of urgency and immediacy. Our research seemed to really matter.

The country was sufficiently small – at that time some four million inhabitants – that it presented a perfect social science laboratory. In those years and in that place disciplines were not impregnable silos but complementary and intersecting perspectives focused on the same object – a nation in transition.

Apart from pursuing a sociology degree I did have another motive in enrolling for an MA at UNZA and that was to learn about the politics of Zambian students. I was the only white student pursuing a degree while living among the undergraduates on campus – an education in itself. I turned my presence on campus into a study of the Zambian student movement. It became my MA thesis – a sprawling 500-page account of the place of Zambian students in the social and political structure that I condensed into a short article a few years later (Burawoy 1976b). My participant observation became a form of public sociology as I partook in campus activism alongside other students. I did not understand that I was playing with fire.

At the time of independence in 1964 there were but 100 university graduates – the new nation needed its own university, a symbol of its independence. It needed its own people to fill the positions occupied by expatriates. When I arrived on campus in 1970, the University of Zambia was only four years old. It had opened with an enrollment of 310 students and by 1970 its enrollment had risen to 1,469. The goal was to increase the number to 5,000. It was a modern concrete structure on the outskirts of the capital, Lusaka. Students saw themselves as a presumptive elite that would eventually replace both the remaining expatriates and the generation of Zambian leaders and professionals reared under colonialism.

The university was integral to Fanon's National Bourgeois Road, a channel of upward mobility. If students deployed contempt for the incumbents of the new ruling class, for the most part, it was not with a view to transforming the class structure but rather for themselves to occupy the ramparts of power. There was a latent and sometimes blatant conflict between the aspirants of two roads into the ruling class – one via the university and educational credentials and the other via the youth wing of the dominant political party, the United National Independence Party (UNIP). Two principles of entitlement were at war: expertise versus loyalty. Each group was contemptuous of the other.

While I was learning sociology from books, from writing papers, from my teachers, I was also learning to practice sociology on a day-to-day basis in the student community. I turned up to the founding meeting of the University of Zambia Sociological Association (UNZASA), and even though I hardly said a word I was unanimously elected chair of the association – whether because of my color or my seniority I do not know. From that position I led a series of dangerous and problematic ventures. In the name of UNZASA we began inviting leading politicians and ministers to the campus. They knew they were entering a cauldron of hostility, but they were fearless, brilliant orators. They would stir things up by berating students for their arrogance and sense of entitlement. Students returned the compliment by turning their wrath on what they believed to be corrupt politicians betraying the public trust. UNZASA ran opinion polls that sought to define the student oppositional consciousness – polls that only confirmed the worst suspicions of UNIP's political leaders. I would write columns for the student newspaper, *UZ*, that often drew on the ideas of Fanon. You might say this was taking observant participation too far – or you might say this was a form of organic public sociology. In Latin America they called it *participant action research*.

In an annual ritual, students would organize a protest outside one of the foreign embassies – usually British or French – for their support of apartheid South Africa. It was always a protest that began in support of government policy. Zambia, after all, was one of the front-line states providing a home for the exiled African National Congress (the banned opposition party to apartheid) and, as a result, bearing the brunt of hostilities from South Africa. In 1970 I was absent from the protest, having a prior engagement on the Copperbelt, and so fellow students began to question my loyalties. The following year I made sure I was marching with them – this time against the French Embassy, protesting the sale of Mirage jet fighters to South Africa. That year the protest turned into a battle with the police. Decked out in riot gear, they took to disbanding the students with tear gas. Students fought back and several arrests were made, including myself, an all too visible white protestor. We were in jail for a few hours before being released on our own recognizance, with a trial to follow. Having joined forces with the protesting students, I became an instant hero.

Infuriated by the police response to their demonstration of support for government policy, student leaders turned on President Kaunda, publicly exposing secret letters he had been exchanging with the South African Prime Minister, John Vorster. From the standpoint of the ruling party, students constituted an unruly opposition. Such flagrant attacks on the most sacred of national symbols – President Kaunda himself – could not go unpunished. UNIP Youth marched on the university in protest against the students, and that night the police, supported by the military, invaded the campus. We were herded out of our dorms at gunpoint and the following day the Chancellor declared the university closed. Two expatriate lecturers were expelled, accused of inciting students and spreading subversive ideas – convenient scapegoats to explain the disloyalty of students.

When the university reopened three months later, the political atmosphere on campus had been transformed. The party had infiltrated the student body, instigating the creation of a UNIP Branch on campus, designed to monitor and regulate student politics. Previously free of party politics, the campus was now divided between UNIP supporters and those of the opposition party, the United

Progressive Party (UPP). The conflict had a strong ethnic coloring, as the UPP was based in the Copperbelt, the home of the Bemba people. We ran another opinion poll on student reaction to the closure of the university and the expulsion of the lecturers. The opposition sentiments, clearly expressed in the results, only exacerbated hostilities between government and students. UNIP students turned on me, attacking me as a secret agent of South Africa. I was already on my way out – a fitting but depressing end to my involvement in Zambian student politics.

Traditional public sociologists can hide behind the protection of the university and its safeguard of free speech and autonomy – where they exist. Organic public sociologists, on the other hand, give up such autonomy when they immerse themselves in their community of engagement. They become vulnerable to forces they don't control. Being directly accountable to those one studies can be a matter of life and death, as sociologists have found in the dictatorships of Africa, Latin America, and elsewhere – dictatorships that can threaten the very existence of sociology as civil society is eclipsed.

My experience in Zambia was at once exhilarating and sobering. Social change does not come easily and when it does occur it cannot be easily engineered. It often takes place behind one's back. Sociology had begun to provide me with the tools to understand those occult forces: how they operate within a context, a field of contestation among actors who mobilize power in pursuit of their interests. I was still groping for theories that might help me better understand what that field looks like, who were the actors in it, how they mobilized power, and what shaped their interests.

But theories are not simply ways of organizing research, differing in their explanatory power. They also have political significance. Theories become actors in the political arena: ideologies that justify the existing array of institutions, constellations of interests, and the distribution of power; utopias that grip people's imagination and thereby propel collective action. Theories animated the ruling class's perspective on development, the corporation's abstention from politics, and student engagement in politics. Both as scientific schemes and as political forces, theories become the necessary backdrop of any public sociology. I needed to learn about theory.

Part Four
Critical Sociology

The 1960s and 1970s were awash with theories of modernization that urged Africa and other postcolonial nations to advance by following the course of Western development. Indeed, leaders of many new nations tried to replicate that history by implanting Western institutions – a combination of markets, planning, and democracy. When these transplants failed to put down roots, modernization theory argued that the soil was too infertile, that Africa was too stuck in its past, inheriting an indelible culture inimical to development. In Zambia I learned the flaws in this theory, and that there were other forces holding back development.

It was there that I first read the compelling Marxist critiques of modernization theory by a Latin Americanist, Andre Gunder Frank (1966), on the development of underdevelopment – that is, the development of the metropolis comes at the expense of the periphery. This meant that the Third World cannot advance without cutting itself off from the First World. As I left Zambia, other treatises were in preparation and about to appear. Walter Rodney's (1972) account of how Europe underdeveloped Africa was published; the Egyptian social scientist Samir Amin (1974) was advancing his theory of accumulation on a world scale. These critical works underlay Immanuel Wallerstein's (1974) world systems theory that argued that it was one thing to be the first nation to develop capitalism, it was quite another to develop capitalism in the midst of already established and powerful capitalist nations.

One epicenter of this rising Marxism was in the neighboring country of Tanzania at the newly created University of Dar es Salaam. Encouraged by President Nyerere and his socialist visions, there emerged a Marxist school of social science led by such figures as Walter Rodney, John Saul, Mahmood Mamdani, Giovanni Arrighi, and Issa Shivji. They examined the internal obstacles to development posed by class structure and class interests inherited from colonialism. These were all critiques of capitalism that, in one way or another, pointed to an as-yet-unrealized socialism. The Marxists were making a double critique: of capitalism itself and the ideologies that justified it.

My Zambian teachers and research had cultivated in me an academic habitus with an irreversible Marxist disposition. But I was also drawn to Marxism's Siamese twin – sociology – that I had absorbed as part of my training. At this point sociology was still largely immune to the Marxist virus, though new strains coming from the Global South were making inroads. Apart from a nostalgia lingering from my earlier visit to the US, I wanted to tackle modernization theory on its home terrain. I wanted to understand how conservative sociology had become such a powerful influence the world over. I, therefore, paid another call on my benefactor, Edward Shils, seeking to revive his proposal that I undertake a PhD in the US. With his help I managed to scrape into the PhD program at the University of Chicago. Perhaps he thought my errant ways would be rectified in the punitive atmosphere of that esteemed university. Still, I was a risky prospect, so I received no financial support. I thought that my mathematics degree, that had proven to be so useful in Zambia, would at least get me a research assistantship. But the head of the National Opinion Research Center, located at the university, told me there was nothing doing and it would be a mistake for me to enroll in the program. Ignoring his advice, I sank my Copperbelt savings into Chicago's PhD program. Given my interests in Africa and India, Chicago seemed to be an appropriate place – the home of the Committee on New Nations that had been dominated by such anthropologists as Clifford Geertz and Lloyd Fallers, as well as sociologists Morris Janowitz and, of course, Edward Shils himself. But I arrived too late. By 1972 the Committee on New Nations had been disbanded and the interest in "new nations" was more or less abandoned, at least in sociology.

After the excitement of the interdisciplinary seminars at the University of Zambia, sociology at Chicago proved to be decidedly tedious, smugly complacent in its provincialism. There was certainly not a sniff or a whiff of Marxism. Critical sociologists had been forcibly removed three years before I arrived: Dick Flacks and Marlene Dixon had been let go and radical students had been expelled. It was not all darkness, however. There were one or two bright lights in the sociology department – Richard Taub, who taught political sociology, and Barry Schwartz, who taught social psychology. But, for me, William Julius Wilson was the brightest light. Without his support – moral, political, and material – I would not have survived Chicago sociology and I would not be writing this book.

Bill encouraged me to pursue my interest in South Africa's racial order. So I delved into the South African historiography, as it was then, very much influenced by my teachers in Zambia and, in particular, by the appearance of Jack and Ray Simons's *Class and Colour in South Africa, 1850–1950* in 1969. Centered as it was on the relation between class and race, their approach was glaringly different from the existing US sociology of race, which was struggling to extricate itself from race cycle theories, assimilation theses, and prejudice studies. Through Bill I was introduced to an insurgent paradigm of racial domination, sparked by the civil rights movement. Though representing relations between white and Black as a relationship of domination was a radical move for

US sociology, it remained far behind the historical studies of South Africa that examined the dynamics of race and class. Accordingly, I embarked on my first critique of US sociology – its limited vision of "race relations" (Burawoy 1974).

As I was struggling with a cumbersome Marxist framework of "base" and "superstructure," Adam Przeworski set me on new paths. A new professor in political science, he introduced me to the then-fashionable French structuralist Marxism. His seminar on Marxist theories of the state transformed the way I thought about theory, and Marxism in particular. In Adam's seminar I developed a Marxist approach to migration that centered on the role of the state. My interest in migration had been first stimulated by my teacher Jaap van Velsen, who saw circulatory labor migration in Southern Africa as a function of capitalism's search for cheap labor. I wanted to advance Jaap's ideas by showing that labor migration was not a peculiar attribute of "backward" Africa but could also be found in advanced capitalism. Thus, I explored the parallel system of migrant labor that was the foundation of California agribusiness (Burawoy 1976a). The study calls into question not only the foundations of modernization theory, but also the sociological reduction of migration to independent forces of "push" and "pull." There was no way, I claimed, to study labor migration without also studying its place within capitalism and recognizing the importance of the state.

The third project in critical sociology was my dissertation, which stemmed from my interest in industrial work, first cultivated on the Zambian Copperbelt. Again, the original impetus was to compare workplaces in the Global North and the Global South and to show that such differences as existed were the product of capitalism on a world scale. My research took place in the midst of the renaissance of Marxism and, in particular, the rediscovery of the "labor process" inspired by Harry Braverman's *Labor and Monopoly Capital* (1974) – a historical examination of the transformation of capitalist work, a rewriting of Marx's Volume One of *Capital*. Industrial sociology had been dominated by employer concerns about the "restriction of output." The quiescence of labor in the 1950s and 1960s, however, had thrown industrial sociology into abeyance, creating the vacuum into which Marxism marched. I focused my attention not on "restriction of output," but on the opposite, the inexplicable intensity with which workers devoted themselves to production or, in Marxist terms, how it was that workers actively participated in their own exploitation. The book that emerged from the dissertation was called *Manufacturing Consent* (1979).

Each in their own way, these three studies challenged conventional sociology: the euphoria of race relations theory that assumed racism was either skin deep or had its own self-sustaining autonomy, the ethnocentrism of modernization theory that deemed Africa to be responsible for its own "backwardness," and the instrumentalism of industrial sociology as an arm of management. In each case my critique was embedded in an open-ended, experimental Marxism that opposed utopianism with the anti-utopian structuralism then current in Marxist circles. After leaving graduate school I would draw on these three studies to explore the distinctive features of South Africa's racial capitalism – how the state enforced a system of brutalizing labor migration alongside a system of racial despotism in the workplace. Inspired by the new historiography of South Africa, I showed the limitations of a widely held sociology of race as seen through the lens of class – namely, Edna Bonacich's theory of the "split labor market." I devote the fourth and last chapter on critical sociology to my long essay originally titled "The Capitalist State in South Africa" (Burawoy 1981).

7

Race, Class, and Colonialism

William Julius Wilson and I joined Chicago's sociology department at the same time. Arriving from the University of Massachusetts as a newly appointed associate professor, he became the only African American on the sociology faculty. Bill had just finished his first book, *Power, Racism, and Privilege* (1973), and was already thinking about his second book, *The Declining Significance of Race* (1978), which would bring him fame, controversy, and a luminescent career like none other in sociology. His skepticism toward affirmative action, with its implicit critique of the African American bourgeoisie, won him many enemies and friends he did not desire. As I have already indicated, in celebrated book after celebrated book he would stick to his guns, exposing different dimensions of the class divisions within the African American population, but with a focus on the poverty and plight of the "underclass." When he first took up a position in Chicago's sociology department his future trajectory, however, was only in gestation.

That first quarter in the fall of 1972, he gave a course on race relations. I enrolled with enthusiasm. It was the highlight of my first year. He was presenting the power conflict perspective, advanced in his first book that was soon to appear. Racism has to be understood as a relation of domination, white over Black – an argument that was gaining credibility at the time, reflecting the experience and influence of the civil rights movement. Bill defined successive racial orders in the US – a move from slavery and Jim Crow segregation based on biological racism to the contemporary period of competitive race relations based on cultural racism. The opening of opportunities for the Black middle classes encouraged renewed protest. The last chapters were devoted to a comparison of "race relations" in South Africa and the United States. Thinking of my own work in Zambia and South Africa, while listening to his lectures, I was struck by the absence of any serious talk of class, within both Black and white races. My unflagging interruptions were undoubtedly very annoying, but Bill was interested. He was thinking along similar lines.

I was lucky Bill did not have the legions of students he would subsequently acquire and so we entered into an extended dialogue about race and class. He read my monograph, *The Colour of Class on the Copper Mines*, and encouraged me to work on the history of South Africa's racial order and a critique of the US sociology of "race relations." Indeed, I was quite astonished by the continuing currency of antiquated approaches – race cycle theories that ended happily, assimilation theses and prejudice studies – as though racism would simply evaporate with time or attitude change. This illusory view, a legacy of the uncritical optimism of US sociology, needed a heavy dose of anti-utopianism. And so it came with the power resource models of sociologists such as Hubert Blalock's (1967) racial threat theory and Bob Blauner's (1972) popularization of the internal colonial model. Still, the problem with these models was their failure to examine the broader economy, and thus the relationship between class and race; and their limited model of social change based, as it was, on an indeterminate conflict between racial groups. They still took race as given, rather than forged in the fire of capitalism.

I developed a very different approach to racial orders. Inspired by Giovanni Arrighi's (1967) account of Southern

Rhodesia's political economy and Jack and Ray Simons's (1969) foundational treatise, I divided South African history into four periods, each marked by an expanding capitalism that transformed the racial configuration of the class structure. The patterning of race and class within the economy was shaped by a racialized "superstructure" that itself underwent changes over time. History unfolded through the interaction between economy and political and ideological institutions. In Marxist language, it was not that the "superstructure" simply reflected the "economic base," it also reacted back upon the base (Burawoy 1974).

The history I told began in the nineteenth century with the growing mining industry, first diamonds and then gold, that drew on indigenous unskilled African labor and imported British workers who occupied the more skilled and supervisory positions. Dispossessed of their land by Afrikaaner farmers – descended from Dutch settlers – and then subject to taxation by the colonial administration, African peasants were driven into the labor market.

With the expansion of the mining industry, British imperialism clashed with and defeated Afrikaaner landed interests in the Boer War. Now the mining companies threatened to meet increased demand for labor by promoting Africans into positions hitherto monopolized by white workers. Festering hostility to mining capital came to a head with the Rand Revolt of 1922 in which white mineworkers struck under the slogan "Workers of the world fight and unite for a white South Africa." It became a violent conflagration, crushed by government troops, but white workers got their way – the entrenchment of an industrial color bar, reserving certain jobs for whites only. In agriculture Africans eked out a subsistence existence while segregated from an emerging class of landless, poor whites. The latter, largely Afrikaaners, were caught between prosperous white landowners and dispossessed Black peasants. In towns Afrikaaners could not compete with cheap African labor, instigating a "civilized labor policy," which promised them jobs in a growing public sector. Between the two world wars, the South African superstructure was consolidating its apparatus of white supremacy.

After World War II, the growth of the manufacturing class led to demands for a permanent Black labor force that was both cheap and skilled. The interests of the manufacturers clashed with an alliance of white landowners and white industrial workers, seeking to defend their racial privileges. The latter alliance was politically victorious and the racial structure of apartheid was erected, with its extensive controls over the social and geographical mobility of Blacks, preventing the emergence of a stabilized Black proletariat. In the rural areas, the apartheid project created Bantustans, internal colonies run by African chiefs with their own bureaucracies, thereby creating dependent African middle classes. The final period of my historical analysis was marked by the rise of a Black bourgeoisie and the dissolution of colonial rule in the rest of Africa. It was then that the apartheid state adopted its outward-looking policy. Driven by internal economic expansion, it sought out markets in newly independent Africa while internally trying to co-opt the new Black middle class.

There was nothing original in the history I offered. Drawing heavily on Simons and Simons (1969), I wanted to demonstrate that you can't study race without attending to class, and that you can't study the political superstructures that constituted race without attending to the dynamics of capitalism. Contrary to optimistic liberal views about the inevitable breakdown of apartheid in the face of an expanding capitalism, the analysis suggested that capitalism, far from being impeded by a racialized superstructure, could effectively expand within and through institutional racism.

I sent this article to various sociology journals and learned my lesson: frontal assault on reigning orthodoxies does not win supportive reviews. It was eventually published in the West Indies. Still, my argument did not go far enough. I'd moved away from psychological theories of racism and race cycle theories, with its stages of competition, conflict, accommodation, and assimilation. I'd moved beyond power-resource models of racial domination to highlight racial divisions within classes and class divisions within races as these evolved with the expansion of capitalism. But I was still missing a *theory* of capitalism.

I extended and formalized the framework I had developed to study race and class in Zambia, but, as in the earlier monograph, I did not have the theoretical tools to incorporate the driving forces behind the pursuit of profit – a systemic analysis of capitalism. That would have to await my second year in graduate school, when I came under the influence of Adam Przeworski. It was then that I read Marx's *Capital* for the first time – an experience from which I've never recovered. Under Adam's guidance I also immersed myself in French structuralist Marxism that had stimulated a new historiography of South Africa, to which I will turn in Chapter 10. First, I had to develop a theory of migrant labor (Chapter 8) and then a theory of the regulation of the workplace (Chapter 9).

8

Migrant Labor and the State

The great South African anthropologist Max Gluckman, founder and director of the Manchester School of Anthropology, would send his doctoral students to Africa with the required reading of two classics of the English industrial revolution, written by J. L. and Barbara Hammond: *The Village Labourer* (1911) and *The Town Labourer* (1917). Students were to read them on the long boat journey – this was the 1950s – so they should not get transfixed by the exoticism of Africa, but see it through the lens of the English industrial revolution. In the same aversion to the "othering" of Africa, when they returned to Manchester after completing their three years of fieldwork, Gluckman would expect them to undertake an ethnography of some institution or organization that was parallel to the one they studied in Africa. Thus, Victor Turner, perhaps the most famous of Gluckman's students, became entranced by rituals of the Ndembu of Northern Rhodesia, so he was steered into studying the rituals in the Roman Catholic Church – with fateful consequences: from being a committed communist he became a deeply religious Roman Catholic. With it came a new tableau of cultural anthropology.

This lesson has never left me. Too much of social science is fragmented into area studies, making it impossible to compare across areas, to compare less developed with more developed countries. How often have I heard colleagues declare a particular comparison across areas as inadmissible. You can't compare Israel and Serbia, they would declare, that's apples and oranges. But in comparing apples and oranges, we can demonstrate that they are both species of fruit and thereby learn things about both that had been beyond a fruitless methodology. The challenge of the sociological imagination is precisely to compare the incomparable. But we should do it systematically. Too often social science runs with unstated, implicit comparisons: the reality of one place with a stereotype or idealization of another – the reality of Africa (dictatorship, corruption, tribalism) against the idealization of the US (democracy, freedom, justice). To reveal these assumptions makes them laughable, so they are generally left implicit. There's a simple principle here: first, compare reality with reality, to establish the commonality between phenomena in different countries, and only *then* ask in what ways they differ and why. Out of this arises sociology with global dimensions. This methodological strategy inspired my comparison of migrant labor in South Africa and California, as well as many dissertations I directed.[2]

As I have said my interest in migrant labor began with my teacher, Jaap van Velsen, who also trained under Max Gluckman. Originally from the Netherlands, he studied the Lakeside Tonga of Malawi in the early 1950s (then Nyasaland). The Tonga claimed to be a matrilineal and matrilocal tribe but, as he discovered, in reality there were many deviations. Whereas other anthropologists had swept such exceptions to kinship rules under the rug, van Velsen (1964) turned them into a "poststructuralist" anthropology in which "norms" are not blindly followed but manipulated in pursuit of interests defined by a broader field of action. In his case, the kinship politics in the village he studied was shaped, at least in part, by labor migration to the South African mines, a thousand miles away. Where others, such as the famous anthropologist Audrey Richards, had claimed the absence of men due to labor migration was destroying the rural economy, van Velsen (1960) showed how the gender division of labor adapted to migration and, together with remittances, strengthened the rural economy. In this way, van Velsen demonstrated how a village in Malawi could not be disentangled from the wider political economy of Southern Africa. While his own field research had been focused on the response of villagers to migration, van Velsen was convinced that the mining industry in South Africa had conspired with the colonial administration in Malawi to turn the latter into a reservoir of African labor. He never found the smoking gun, although that was what became of Malawi.

This was a very different perspective than was current in the "modernization" literature that saw African labor migration – the cyclical movement between town and country – as a function of the primordial attachments to tribe and kinship. In that account, Africans couldn't free themselves from the heavy weight of tradition. Van Velsen painted a different picture. He saw labor migration as a function of capitalism's search for cheap labor power: laborers need only be paid a wage for their individual survival while the costs of rearing the family would be borne by the sending community. This separation between what I call "maintenance" and "renewal" of labor power was orchestrated and enforced by the South African state that taxed the rural population, thereby compelling them to seek wage labor (Burawoy 1976a). At the same time, the South African state outlawed permanent residence in the urban areas, so workers had to return periodically to their home villages. Under the influence of van Velsen, Giovanni Arrighi (1970) studied the history of capitalism in Southern Rhodesia. He was the first to elaborate the political economy approach to labor migration, before he became a distinguished sociologist of world systems.

My ideas were also influenced by Harold Wolpe. A South African freedom fighter in exile in England and a member of the South African Communist Party, he became a sociologist at a time when Marxism was flourishing in UK universities. In 1972 Wolpe published his seminal article on labor migration within South Africa, arguing that the racial order of apartheid emerged from the state's design to produce cheap labor power for capital by recreating the reserves, later called Bantustans. There African families – women, elderly men, and children – were supposed to cultivate a subsistence existence while able-bodied men were compelled to migrate to the mines on short-term contracts. The racial order was not at odds with capitalism, as liberal historiography and modernization theory claimed. Rather it functioned to reproduce capitalism, not by dividing the working class but through the detailed regulation of both the social and geographical mobility of African labor. Further, Wolpe (1972) argued, with land erosion subsistence existence was made more difficult, and cheap labor could only be secured through political repression – this was the transition from "segregation" to "apartheid."

Wolpe's article as well as his subsequent research led to new questions for the Marxist historiography of South Africa (Burawoy 1989, 2004). How was it that the South African state undertook precisely the policies that would produce a distinctive racial capitalism based on Black migrant labor? Was it the result of class struggles by white or Black workers? Did it result from the interest of the state itself in preventing revolutionary ferment in the cities? Was it the effect of the changing relations among different fractions of the capitalist class? A vibrant literature emerged, largely debated by South African scholars living in the UK and influenced by the French Marxism developed across the Channel.

This literature, however, was specific to South Africa. Like modernization theory, it implied that labor migration was a peculiarity of Africa – now associated with the colonial or apartheid state rather than the cultural backwardness of Africans. In studying migrant labor, I had another goal – to examine how far this framework applied to advanced capitalism. I wanted to show that similar patterns of labor migration with similar "functions" could be found elsewhere. Indeed, at that time social scientists were beginning to study labor migration to Germany, France, and the UK. Manuel Castells (1975) had attributed the cheapness and thus appeal of migrant labor to its political weakness relative to established labor. I argued that the cheapness of migrant labor lay, first and foremost, in its material basis, namely, the forcible separation of maintenance from renewal. My case was California.

At the end of my first year in Chicago, fellow graduate student Ida Susser and I went off in search of Mexican migrant laborers employed by Californian agribusiness. It turned out that this was a period of escalating class struggle organized by the United Farm Workers and there were strikes across the fields. At that time the United Farm Workers had mounted a very successful nationwide grape boycott and had been making substantial challenges to agribusiness. I began thinking of the similarities and differences between the "systems" of migrant labor in South African mining and Californian agriculture. In both cases workers came from different national or ethnic labor forces: in South Africa from the artificially created Bantustans and neighboring countries; in California from a succession of imported ethnic-national labor forces, one succeeding the next as they abandoned agriculture for more stable employment.

The Bracero Program that imported single laborers on contract from Mexico was the prototype for the production of cheap labor power – with their families back in Mexico, men worked the fields for low wages but still enough to send remittances back home. Those same laborers couldn't settle in California, but were forced back to Mexico at the end of their contracts. The Bracero Program ended in 1964 and a new regime of migrant labor was installed that rested on "undocumented" labor. This might be said to parallel Wolpe's shift from "segregation" to "apartheid" (Paret 2011). Still, there seemed to be a difference. While in South Africa migrant labor had a systemic character, definitive of the entire racial order, in California it was of a more conjunctural character, with agribusiness taking advantage of labor reserves in a neighboring country, aided and abetted by the state.

The study not only advanced a comparative analysis of systems of labor migration; it was also designed to debunk stereotypes about Africa and Africans. Circulating migrant labor was not a function of traditional African culture or weak labor commitment but of the coercive regimes of collaboration between capital and the state that forced workers into migratory patterns. Such regimes could be found elsewhere in the world, not just under colonialism. Moreover, I showed that theories developed in Africa could generate new insights into social phenomena found in advanced capitalism. The reigning theories of migration at the time were based on "push and pull" factors, treated as independent forces. Such theories, largely pioneered by demographers, missed the critical role of states operating in reproducing systems of cheap labor. It would bring the study of migrant labor to the heart of Marxism – the relationship between capitalism, labor, and the state. How is cheap labor produced? Cheap for whom? It could be cheap for capital but expensive for the state, as it takes on complex functions to regulate the social and geographical mobility of labor.

This framework has since been advanced in different directions. The first critical move was to undertake ethnographies at both ends of the migration stream. I still remember the excitement of reading Pierrette Hondagneu-Sotelo's MA thesis on Mexican migration to California that explored the connection between the sending community and the receiving community. Her dissertation made two more critical moves: the centering of gender in patterns of migration and a more nuanced understanding of the role of the receiving state. Thus, she investigated the strategies of households in organizing the migration of men and women and how this changed with the new immigration policies of the US state (Hondagneu-Sotelo 1994).

But it was also important to understand the role of the sending state. Thus, Sheba George (2005) studied state-regulated migration of Kerala nurses to Chicago, showing how women came first and men followed, giving rise to a gender reversal of domestic roles. Robyn Rodriguez (2010) focused on the way the Philippine state orchestrates the training and distribution of laborers across the globe, and how consequently the Philippine state becomes the object of struggle by which laborers seek to protect themselves from inhumane employers. Andy Chang (forthcoming) takes the program further, studying how, together with labor brokers, sending *and* receiving states organized gendered streams of migration from Indonesia to Taiwan, but with the added complication that both states were embedded in competitive relations with yet other states. One cannot understand a migration pattern between two countries without embedding it in the multilateral relations among states competing to send or attract migrants.

Recent research has become more ambitious, comparing migration streams from different communities within the same country. Abigail Andrews (2018) followed migrants from different villages in Mexico with different destinations in California – in the one case a more linear pattern sustained by a community bound by traditional mores and in the other case a more circular pattern in which gender norms were reconstituted. Aya Fabros is studying two villages in the Philippines, one concentrating on sending migrants to Italy as domestic workers and the other sending migrants to different countries in the Middle East. She shows how the sending and receiving communities are mutually constitutive so as to form two systems of migration shaped by the relations among states. Cinzia Solari (2017) compared the circular migration of single women between Ukraine and Italy, where they became homecare workers, with unidirectional family migration of Ukrainian families to California. The migrants to Italy were grandmothers, displaced from caregiving by their daughters, who had lost their jobs in the post-communist economic collapse. In each study it was important to explore the interaction of sending and receiving states. A student of Michael Piore, Natasha Iskander (2010) compares Mexico and Morocco, grappling with the developmental contribution of migrant labor through the sending state's promotion of remittances and investment in the home community.

The same theoretical framework can work for internal migration. As in apartheid South Africa, the Chinese state organized the circular migration of workers between town and country through the *hukou* system, a variant of the South African pass laws, which made permanent urban residence difficult for rural migrants (Alexander and Chan 2004). Julia Chuang (2020) studied this system from the perspective of the rural regions, showing how it was being destabilized by a new mode of accumulation based on land expropriation that eroded the basis of cheap labor power.

My own comparison between California and South Africa began as a critical sociology, critical of modernization theory for its ethnocentric assumptions and demographers for their models of push and pull factors. It blossomed into a full-fledged political economy, stimulated by the turn to the state in the renaissance of Marxism. Today, no one can possibly ignore the role of the state in studying migratory labor, and it has become part and parcel of an exciting research program.

9

Manufacturing Consent

It was 1973, the beginning of my second year at the University of Chicago. I was wandering around the bookstore, looking at the titles that had been ordered for different courses. There, much to my astonishment, were a set of books for a course on Marxism – Gramsci's *Selections from the Prison Notebooks*; Nicos Poulantzas, *Political Power and Social Classes*; Louis Althusser, *For Marx*; Althusser and Etienne Balibar, *Reading Capital*. I knew about these books but I had never read them. What were they doing here at the University of Chicago? I decided to find out. I was not the only one. Indeed, it seemed the whole university wanted to squeeze into a small room in Pick Hall where Adam Przeworski was to give a graduate seminar on the "state."

Originally trained in Poland as a sociologist, he took his PhD in political science from Northwestern University. His first job was at Washington University in St. Louis and he had now just arrived to take up a position in the political science department at Chicago. He came fresh from a sabbatical year in Paris where he had been captivated by the fashionable Marxism – the same French structuralism that had inspired the new historiography of South Africa. He was now interpreting this abstract theorizing through the lens of the great Italian Marxist, Antonio Gramsci. This was the most exhilarating seminar I would ever take.

It was populated by students from different disciplines and from different countries, united by their interest in Marxism. It was led by the brilliant, chain-smoking Polish professor, who thought and spoke with arrowhead clarity, parsimony, and elegance about the stubborn resilience of capitalism. He was in the midst of developing a theory of capitalist democracy, both its limitations and its necessity, which would later bring him much fame (Przeworski 1985).

As the course proceeded it struck me that there were uncanny parallels between the still-influential "structural functionalism" pioneered by Talcott Parsons and this newfangled Marxist "structuralism." They were both concerned with questions of what keeps society going, and what the moral or ideological bases of continuity were. Tired of hearing my remonstrations and, perhaps, a little intrigued by their convergence and therefore all the more interested in their divergence, Adam invited me to teach a course with him on Marxism and functionalism. We would alternate between presentations on the works of Marx and Engels, Althusser and Poulantzas, on the one hand, and the works of Talcott Parsons on the other. Out of this engagement emerged my first attempt at a full-fledged Marxist critique of sociology, which I would take with me into my dissertation. Critique requires one to take the object of criticism very seriously, understanding its inner logic as well as its outer determination.

The so-called Chicago School, known for its ethnographies of urban life, was in remission. There had been a time when Chicago sociology, under the leadership of Everett Hughes and William Foote Whyte (both long since departed), had encouraged participant observation studies of the industrial enterprise. For my dissertation I resolved to return to that lost tradition but with a Marxist lens.

So I went in search of a blue-collar job. That was easier said than done. No one wanted to employ a useless graduate student without industrial skills. But eventually, with the help of a relative, I landed a job in Allis-Chalmers,

the large multinational corporation that produced agricultural and construction equipment, a competitor to John
Deere and International Harvester. Headquartered in
Milwaukee, the company's engine division was located
south of Chicago, in Harvey, Illinois, which is where I
began as a machine operator on July 2 of 1974. I worked
there for nearly a year, my incompetence endangering
the lives of my fellow workers as well as my own. As a
middle-class lad I had no experience of blue-collar life,
either at work or at home. From the beginning I was
impressed by how much skill there was in a supposedly
unskilled job; and also by how hard people worked, for
no obvious reason. This was the puzzle that defined my
study – why did workers work so hard, sweating to make
the rates for the job, making a few extra crumbs so that
capitalists would make more profit? Indeed, how did even
I – skeptical though I was – get absorbed in trying to
"make out"? What I observed seemed to rub up against
the picture painted by industrial sociology that was
obsessed with the opposite question: Why are workers so
indolent? Or to put it in more technical language, why do
they "restrict output"? Taking the managerial standpoint,
sociologists and industrial relations experts had always
asked why workers don't work harder, or studied how to
get them to work harder ... but that didn't tally with what
I saw on the shop floor.

Not just experientially, but also theoretically, my
question seemed to be the more obvious one. Marxism,
after all, has to explain how it is that workers produce
more value through their labor than is embodied in their
wage. Hitherto Marxists assumed, along with Marx, that
it was the economic whip of the market, the fear of being
fired, that explained hard work. If not that, then it was the
economic incentive that drove workers. These factors were
undeniably at play – but at Allis-Chalmers it was quite
difficult to be fired and we were guaranteed a minimum
wage. Coercion, by itself, could not explain my fellow
workers' enthusiasm, their ingenuity, and their devotion to

hard work. It was especially intriguing because whenever I asked them why they worked so hard, machine operators were dumb-founded, convinced that this was not the case! It was a badge of honor to claim that that they were not collaborating with management, but there they were killing themselves to make the rate.

While I was working at Allis, Harry Braverman's *Labor and Monopoly Capital* (1974) appeared. A reconstruction and update of Volume 1 of Marx's *Capital*, it became an instant classic, drawing attention to the capitalist labor process. Braverman rewrote the history of the transformation of work based on the principle of deskilling – what he called the separation of conception from execution – that had the double advantage of lowering wages and intensifying managerial control. Bravermania overtook so many of us at the time, but there was a problem. He focused on the "objective" processes of work transformation, not the "subjective" response of workers. Like Marx, he assumed that the coerciveness of the capitalist labor process explained the intensity of work. This seemed decidedly unsatisfactory to me, working at Allis.

Workers faced a stark reality: coming to the plant on time for eight or more hours each day for arduous, repetitive, and intrinsically meaningless work. To make time pass more quickly, to inject meaning into their lives on the shop floor, they turned work into a game called "making out." Making their quotas became a challenge that they pursued through ingenious ways of cutting corners and combining jobs. It was a social game because we were so dependent on the cooperation of an array of auxiliary workers – inspectors, the set-up men, crib attendants, truck drivers. It was also a game against management – or so it appeared. The rules of making out required that you never handed in more than 125 percent of the stipulated managerial norm for each job, although you could bank accumulated work for a rainy day. On difficult jobs we would hand in far less than the 100 percent norm, as if to say to managers they needed to recalibrate the rate. These rules were patrolled by fellow workers. At the end of the shift we would announce to one another our triumphs or defeats, eliciting awe or sympathy as the case may be. The game drew us into the labor process, time passed more quickly, and there developed a culture that bound each to the other. We were emotionally invested in making out – a game that had a life of its own, inherited from generation to generation. We accepted the rules and the conditions of production as given, so the game had the effect of not only *securing* surplus for the capitalist but *obscuring* the capitalist conditions – the relations of production – that made it seductive.

To draw people in, games must be possessed of uncertainty, but neither too little nor too much. Too little uncertainty means the challenge has gone; too much uncertainty means the challenge is too great. Apart from the constitution of the labor process as a game, there were other features of the factory that furthered the conditions of making out. Workers were constituted as individuals – industrial citizens with rights and obligations defined by the grievance machinery, established by the union contract. If management violated the terms of the contract, then it could be held accountable by the union. I called this regulatory order the *internal state*.

Workers were also given rights to compete for job vacancies through an open bidding system, with management selecting new incumbents on the basis of their seniority and experience. This "internal labor market" gave workers limited but real autonomy and even the illusion of power, based on leverage vis-à-vis their foremen who, if they wanted to keep them, had to treat operators with kid gloves or they would move off their job to another one. It also gave workers interest in staying at the enterprise, as seniority brought many rewards – both material and symbolic. If they moved to another union shop they'd have to start at the bottom.

There was another game that set the conditions of making out – the contract negotiations between union and management. This took the form of a class compromise in which higher profits would trickle down in the form of wage increases. The games on the shop floor that got people to work hard could, therefore, deliver long-term benefits for all – expanding production made it possible to coordinate the material interests of workers and capital. In these ways workers were persuaded to devote themselves to produce surplus value for the capitalist – organizing consent to capitalism. The institutions that combined to guarantee consent – labor process as a game, the internal labor market, and the internal state – I called the *hegemonic regime of production*, following the ideas of Antonio Gramsci. But what were the external conditions that made this regime possible?

I was able to tease out the answer due to a strange coincidence: I had landed in the very same factory that had brought fame to one of Chicago's greatest ethnographers. Donald Roy had been a machine operator in that factory – then Buda Company – exactly thirty years earlier, 1944–45. From the start my experiences reminded me of Roy's account of his workplace, analyzed in his published articles. So I turned to his 500-page dissertation, held in Chicago's Regenstein Library (Roy 1952). Even though Roy concealed the identity of his workplace, I knew enough about the history of my plant to realize I had landed in the very same place. No less strange was the similarity in work organization and technology. Apart from a few numerically controlled machines, we were laboring on the same sort of machines as thirty years ago.

My first reaction was panic – what else was there to say? Roy had said it all. His skills as a fieldworker and as an industrial worker put mine to shame. Before coming to graduate school he had been a blue-collar worker most of his adult life – he was as at home on the shop floor as I was at sea there. My second reaction was to use this as an opportunity to attack his theoretical framework as myopic, deriving as it did from the old industrial sociology that insulated the enterprise from its environment – a hallmark, indeed, of Chicago ethnography in general.

When I calmed down I realized that a more fruitful approach would be to undertake a study of the changes in the labor process over time. I could thereby exploit the chance occurrence of a revisit, but also the common technology and piece-rate system. I could therefore pinpoint changes quite precisely. In Roy's day conflicts between management and workers, often mediated by the time-and-study man searching for jobs with loose rates, were more intense, while those between machine operators and auxiliary or service workers were less pronounced. The rights of workers as well as collective bargaining were less developed than thirty years later. I characterized the change as being along the continuum from despotism to hegemony, a shift in the balance of coercion and consent. I then traced this transition to the external environment: first, to the plant's move from the competitive sector to the monopoly sector with its captive markets and, second, to the rise of state-regulated industrial relations, especially where trade unions were recognized.

It seemed that capitalism had developed a foolproof way of perpetuating itself by absorbing challenges and manufacturing consent. Contrary to Marxist thinking of the time, the disorganization of the working class took place not only in the realm of superstructures, through education, parties, religion, community, and family, but at the very point of production where class consciousness was supposed to congeal. Thinking that this hegemonic regime of production would be the bedrock of stability under advanced capitalism, I looked to the Global South for patterns of destabilization that might give concrete expression to utopian visions.

I did not realize how fragile was the hegemonic regime. I did not anticipate that both market and state were undergoing or about to undergo major transformation. Markets were becoming global; Allis-Chalmers would have to compete with foreign enterprises, a competition it did not survive. The state would soon strike up an offensive against labor that would subvert the union movement. Nor did I appreciate how the hegemonic regime had effectively stripped workers of their collective capacity to resist the imposition of new forms of despotism, the mean and lean production of the 1980s, what I would later call *hegemonic despotism*.

I would never have been able to develop this interpretation of my ethnography were it not for the Marxism I had imbibed in Adam's seminar. For, in effect, I had taken Marxist theories of the state, in particular those developed by French structuralism, to the workplace where an "internal state" and "internal labor market" were at work – constituting workers as industrial citizens and organizing a class compromise between capital and labor. In combination these two factors were the conditions for the manufacture of consent. This line of argument was further stimulated by Gramsci's unexplicated remark that in the US "hegemony was born in the factory" (1971: 285). Theory was essential to my interpretation of life on the shop floor – a theory that led me in a very different direction from the industrial sociology of the 1950s, when Roy was writing his dissertation.

As I was later to learn, while I was working away at Allis-Chalmers, Erik Wright was following parallel ideas at Berkeley where he was then a graduate student. Together with other Berkeley students Erik had developed a course on Marxist social science, which he would elaborate and teach on a regular basis for the next forty years. He, too, was opposing mainstream sociology with Marxist analysis. For his dissertation (Wright 1979) he undertook a statistical analysis of survey data to demonstrate the explanatory power of a Marxist theory of class that was rooted in *relations of production*, relations between those who own the means of production and those who don't, that is, between *capitalists* and *workers*. However, he added a third category, "the petty bourgeoisie" – individuals who owned their own means of production but didn't employ wage laborers (self-employed workers such as shopkeepers, or independent craft workers). This gave him three more categories, intermediary between the three fundamental class positions: *managers* between capitalists and wage-laborers (whether low-level supervisors or high-level heads of department); *semi-autonomous workers* between wage laborers and petty bourgeoisie (teachers, lawyers, doctors, etc.); and *small employers* (between capitalists and petty bourgeoisie). He called these intermediary positions "contradictory class locations." He showed how this innovative Marxist analysis was superior to the sociological models of status attainment that strung occupations on a continuum and to the economic models based on human capital – superior, that is, in its capacity to explain variations in income inequality. This would be the beginning of an enormous research program, developing its own survey instrument that included subjective correlates of class and was fielded in more than a dozen countries across the globe (Wright 1985, 1997).

While Erik was developing his analysis of national class structures based on relations *of* production, I was focused on a micro-analysis of the firm, and in particular on the relations *in* production. Where he worked with national-level data to infer what was happening in production, I moved in the opposite direction, from the micro-processes of production to the macro conditions of their existence.

Erik and I suffered from illusions of grandeur. We aimed to replace sociology – professional sociology – with our new Marxist science. We used the tools of sociology – multivariate statistical analysis and participant observation – against sociology. Our work was definitely not aimed at "publics" beyond sociology, but we naïvely assumed that to transform sociology would have real effects, would in and of itself pose a challenge to capitalism. When I worked at Allis-Chalmers I was not interested in influencing my fellow workers, whether converting them to Marxism or helping them build a stronger union. My goal was to use my experiences on the shop floor as the basis for a Marxist critique and supersession of sociology. My audience was other sociologists who were similarly disaffected by reigning paradigms, and who saw the potential of a reconstructed Marxism. The infusion of critical thinking – whether Marxism, feminism, or critical race theory – did give professional sociology a new vitality, and pushed it in new directions.

10

Racial Capitalism

During the 1960s and 1970s Maurice Zeitlin, an ardent if also critical defender of the Cuban Revolution, began his own research program around class analysis. He became an inspirational force for the younger generation like myself – inspirational in the way he combined a radical politics and a Marxist sociology. While a professor at University of Wisconsin–Madison, Maurice mentored several cohorts of graduate students, ready to carry critical perspectives into sociology.[3] In 1977 Maurice left for the University of California–Los Angeles. There he established the annual journal *Political Power and Social Theory* that aimed to meet the highest professional standards of empirical research and, at the same time, to address the big debates of the day through a Marxist or Marxist-inspired lens. It was more academic and less explicitly political than the other leftist journals of the 1970s, journals often run by sociology graduate students, such as *The Insurgent Sociologist*, *Socialist Revolution*, *Berkeley Journal of Sociology*, and *Kapitalistate*.

In 1979, when I was already a junior faculty person at Berkeley, Maurice asked me to review a paper by Edna Bonacich that applied her then well-known "split labor market" theory to South Africa. Edna had been developing her approach to race over the previous decade. It was a major advance over psychological and race cycle theories as well as the power conflict models. It had influenced Bill Wilson as he wrote *The Declining Significance of Race*. However, it suffered from some of the same problems as my own earlier analysis, which I described in Chapter 7, an inadequate theory of capitalism and the state. On reading my review Maurice invited me to write a critical essay (Burawoy 1981) to be published alongside Bonacich's paper (1981).

Edna attributed the peculiarity of South Africa's racial order to the capacity of the white working class to defend its privileged position against the interests of white capital and at the expense of Black labor. She pulled in much evidence to support her claim – indeed, the sort of evidence I had used in my own earlier analysis – but in focusing on the dynamics between high-priced and low-priced labor, Edna not only discounted the contribution of other forces but also left unspecified the very meaning of racial domination.

To talk of racial capitalism, as we do today, is to *situate the analysis of racial domination within an analysis of capitalism*. This means we cannot reduce racial domination to a singular all-embracing "hierarchy"; we have to disentangle the different dimensions of racial domination by paying attention to the meaning of capitalism. In my critique of Bonacich I approached racial domination, therefore, in relation to two sources of capitalist profit: the first through *extracting surplus in the labor process* and the second from lowering *the costs of the reproduction of labor power*, that is, lower wages. I had addressed both sources of profit in my previous work but never connected the two.

To recapitulate the argument from the previous two chapters, in the Marxist scheme, the work day is divided into two analytically distinct parts: *surplus labor*, which is the source of profit, and *necessary labor*, which corresponds to the wage. Furthermore, the value of the wage is the cost of keeping not just the worker alive but also the worker's family, that is to say, maintaining but also renewing the labor force. *Maintenance* and *renewal* refer to the supply of basic needs – foods, clothing, housing – necessary to "reproduce," that is, produce again and again, the present and future capacity of workers to labor, that is, their labor power.

Assuming a competitive market, in pursuing profit the capitalist can, therefore, adopt two strategies. The first strategy is to increase the surplus labor through reorganizing the work process – for example, extending the length of the working day, intensifying work, or introducing new technology. The second strategy is to reduce the necessary labor, which can be accomplished by employing multiple earners per family so that each is paid a lower wage, by capital traveling to places where cost of living is lower and therefore wages are lower, or by cheapening the cost of the materials necessary to keep families alive. Deskilling is an especially appealing strategy, as it accomplishes both the cheapening of the cost of labor power – one can pay deskilled workers less than skilled workers – and increasing surplus, since deskilled workers can be more effectively controlled in the labor process (because of less autonomy and easy replacement).

In apartheid South Africa racial domination is at the center of both strategies. In the extraction of surplus labor in the labor process racial domination takes the form of the color bar – the division between jobs reserved for whites (skilled and supervisory work) and jobs reserved for Blacks (unskilled, semi-skilled, low-level supervision). The regulatory institutions of the workplace denied Blacks rights and gave despotic power to white supervisors to work their Black subordinates to the bone. This system of racial despotism in production rests on clear and explicit limits on occupational mobility, known as *job reservation* – defining what jobs whites can do, what jobs Blacks can do. This despotic order was so different from the hegemonic regime at Allis-Chalmers.

In the reduction of necessary labor, that is, in reducing the costs of the reproduction of labor power, the system of circulating migrant labor was, for a long time, an essential component of the racial order. As I described in Chapter 8, the agricultural communities in the "reservations" or "Bantustans" subsidized low wages in the mines by providing for subsistence existence of women, children, and the elderly. The trick, however, is to maintain the interdependence of the single worker and his origin community while also keeping them geographically separate. This requires a set of laws that regulate the movement of Black wage labor (Pass Laws) and the rights of residence (The Group Areas Act). After their labor contracts have expired, men have to return to their villages, renew relations with their families, and then under the compulsion of taxation and poverty they return to the city for employment. In this way capitalism thrives on the wide-ranging laws that restrict social and geographic mobility and are imposed on Blacks by a racialized state, laws legislated by a majority white parliament. As in Table 10.1 below, racialized restrictions on mobility are the conditions for the possibility of despotism in production and the reproduction of the system of migrant labor.

Table 10.1: The Dimensions of Racial Domination under Racial Capitalism

	Labor Process	Reproduction of Labor Power
Relations between places in the division of labor	Racial despotism in production (color bar)	Separation of maintenance and renewal (migrant labor)
Allocation of races to places in the division of labor	Regulation of occupational mobility (job reservation)	Regulation of geographic mobility (Pass Laws, Group Areas Act)

Source: Author's own

Having established the elements of racial capitalism, we must now ask what are the interests that perpetuate or change this system? For Bonacich, the agent driving the racial order is the white working class. There is ample evidence to suggest that the white working class played a significant role. However, through the lens of even such a simple model of capitalism we can see there is a far more complex set of class interests at work.

First, white workers themselves do not form a homogeneous class fraction. *Skilled white workers* are threatened by deskilling whereas *unskilled white workers* are threatened with replacement by cheaper Black labor. The former have an interest in the color bar and the privileges it confers, so long as it does not erode their monopoly of skills. Unskilled white workers, meanwhile, have an interest in excluding Blacks from employment altogether, and thus in dissolving the color bar.

Second, Bonacich assumes Black labor is inert, yet it too has interests to defend, whether they be against racist laws that enforce migrant labor or draconian treatment in production. Through strikes and stay-aways they make capital, and indirectly white labor, feel their enormous leverage (structural power), a force that will eventually bring down the apartheid order.

Third, just as we have to recognize the diversity of interests within the *dominated* classes, so we have to be careful not to homogenize the *dominant* class. Bonacich does not distinguish between the interests of the individual capitalist, the interests of a fraction of the capitalist class, and the interests of the class as a whole. Individual capitalists face a choice between the erosion of the color bar, which would give them access to cheaper (Black) labor, and retaining the color bar to intensify the extraction of surplus from Black workers. Different fractions of capital have also divergent interests in the racial order. The mining industry has always relied on the recruitment of migrant labor but it had to compete with white (Afrikaaner) farmers, who also depended upon cheap labor from the reserves. As the political power of farmers grew and subsistence agriculture declined with land erosion and over-population, so mining capital was compelled to recruit migrant laborers from neighboring countries. Mining capital has also to be distinguished from manufacturing capital, which grew in strength through the twentieth century. Especially after World War II, manufacturing capital was interested in dissolving the migrant labor system and stabilizing skilled Black labor in the urban areas. Slowly it got its way but at the cost of the massive growth of urban struggles in the 1980s.

Finally, given the divergent interests among these fractions of different classes, how can we explain the specific forms of racial domination? At this point the state, untheorized in Bonacich's account, has to enter the explanation, for it is the state that ultimately creates and enforces the laws that define a racial order. It adjudicates between the interests of different classes and class fractions. How is it, for example, that the state reproduces the system of migrant labor or the color bar or pass laws? In whose interests does the state act and why? Here one has to examine the *capacity* of different groups to enforce their interests, both separately and through alliances – interests that come to be expressed in state interventions even as those interests are themselves constituted by the state. A particular fraction of the dominant class becomes hegemonic, forging a temporary unity both *within* the dominant class as well as *over* the dominated classes. Impelled by the dynamics of capitalism, however, each hegemonic system enters into crisis to be replaced, sooner or later, by another hegemonic order reflecting a different coalition of classes. In this way we are able to develop a periodization of racial capitalism, based on which fraction of capital is hegemonic and whose racial strategies prevail (Davies et al. 1976).

Bonacich's split labor market theory was on to something important, namely, the relation between race and class, perhaps a point of departure but certainly not

a point of conclusion. It confounds levels of analysis –
individual, class fraction, economic class, and political
class; it doesn't discriminate between interests and
capacities, conflates labor market and labor process;
and therefore misses the different arenas and forms of
racial domination. Finally, it doesn't advance a theory
of the state – a relatively autonomous set of institutions
that reproduce the racial order. Without a theory of the
dynamics of capitalism, it cannot discern a succession of
racial orders. It offers an abstract model divorced from
the political and economic context that gives meaning to
racial capitalism. Yet, my own analysis was also flawed.
In trying to understand the unity of capitalism and racism
I missed the very forces that would, within a decade,
unravel apartheid.

The notion of racial capitalism is often traced back
to Du Bois's *Black Reconstruction*. Analyzing the class
structure before the Civil War, he reveals class divisions
within races and the racial divisions within classes – an
arrangement that looks very different in the South and the
North, very different in the US than in other countries,
and different again at the global level. He, too, examines
the succession of different racial orders: the breakdown of
the fragile power-bloc uniting industrialists and planters
triggers the Civil War and the creation of a new racial order
in the South. Reconstruction itself collapses as Northern
capital prompts the withdrawal of military and economic
support for an inter-racial democracy. This leads to the
rise of new forms of forced labor, especially sharecropping
and convict labor, promoting the wages of whiteness – the
psychological and public wage – that laid the basis of a
new order of racial segregation. There are many loose ends
in Du Bois's analysis but his methodology is to excavate
racial capitalism – racial domination examined against
the context of the articulation of slavery and industrial
capitalism on a global scale. Racial capitalism is not a
"thing" but a methodology, situating the study of racism
within an analysis of capitalism.

The abiding achievement of Du Bois was, despite everything, never to lose sight of the possibility of inter-racial collaboration, the possibility of transcending racism as well as capitalism. He never took racism for granted, always examining the historically specific conditions of its reproduction, but always revealing the historical processes through which reproduction leads to transformation. Reading Du Bois today points to the Achilles heel of the Marxist renaissance of the 1970s, so focused on the resilience and durability of capitalism, so rooted in the misplaced optimism of Marx and Engels. Attempts to show that capitalism sowed the seeds of its own destruction, whether due to imminent laws or the deepening of class struggle, were less than convincing. While we recognized that capitalism systematically generated economic crises, these were often regarded as functional, giving capitalism the opportunity to restructure itself. The pluralization of contentious politics in the 1960s – civil rights, anti-war, women's movements – all important in their own right, nonetheless redirected attention away from the project to transcend capitalism. If there was hope it was projected onto the "Third World," where conditions could not sustain a viable capitalism, and socialism was the only alternative. It was a largely unfounded hope, however, since the socialist projects also crumbled in the face of hostile national bourgeoisies aided by a marauding capitalism.

In the final analysis, the critical impulse of Marxist sociology was tamed by its "functionalism" that was consonant with reigning social theory, lubricating our way from critical to professional sociology. At one level, Marxist sociology was, indeed, consistent with the dominant sociology; at another level, it was not. It represented a competing research program, a shift from structural functionalism that spoke of differentiation, modernity, industrialism, and stratification to a Marxism that was grounded in an analysis of capitalism and of class but also race and gender. There was, therefore, a backlash from mainstream sociology. It was a desperate rearguard action to fend off graduate students who were drawn into the newfangled theories that made so much better sense of the world than the consecrated sociology. What were those criticisms from the mainstream, and how did we respond to them?

Part Five
Professional Sociology

The limitations of my naïve policy sociology led me to public sociology; the limitations of my public sociology led me to a critical sociology – a sociology based on the premise that the world could be other than it is, while recognizing there are powerful forces thwarting that possibility. But critical sociology also harbors a critical perspective toward consecrated, professional sociology, complacent in its anti-utopian leanings at the cost of utopian imagination, justifying what exists as natural and inevitable. Why then would a Marxist want to become a professional sociologist?

At the time I was in graduate school, there was a renaissance of Marxism within academia. If there were few signs of such Marxism in Chicago's sociology department, in the neighboring political science and anthropology departments there were Marxist tremors. As I have indicated, in other sociology departments such as Berkeley and Madison, Marxism was a going concern, at least among graduate students. Moreover, I had come from the Third World, as it was then called, where Marxism was flourishing; the same was happening in Western Europe, too. I imagined that if and when I got a job I would be able to advance Marxism through research and through teaching. It was not only that sociology seemed to be a discipline ripe for transformation, but the academic system itself created the spaces for dissident paradigms.

Reflecting on those early years, Erik Wright (1987: 44) later wrote of "visions of glorious paradigm battles with lances drawn and a valiant Marxist knight unseating the bourgeois rival in a dramatic quantitative joust." We both believed that Marxism could stand the test of science. We were politically naïve about the implications of winning such a paradigm battle, thinking it would spontaneously carry over into the world beyond. More immediately, we were sociologically naïve – not appreciating the capacity of the academy to both repress and channel dissent, and how the exigencies of careers can surreptitiously defang radicalism. If we survived would our Marxism survive? It was a risky venture.

Looking back now I'm surprised at how successful we were. In the 1970s and 1980s a cohort of graduate students made its way into tenure-track positions. Marxists were advancing into key departments, especially in the public universities, publishing in flagship journals of the sociology profession as well as creating their own journals. Symptomatic of the times, the *American Journal of Sociology*, one of the two leading professional journals, invited Theda Skocpol and myself to edit a special issue on Marxism (Burawoy and Skocpol 1983). Her instant classic *States and Social Revolutions* (1979) was heavily influenced by Barrington Moore's (1966) brilliant class analysis of different roads to democracy and dictatorship, blazing a trail for young Marxists. While she was deeply ambivalent about Marxism, her early work was inspired by Marxist debates of the time.

The trajectories of this upstart generation were rarely uncontested. Skocpol herself entered a determined, extended, and eventually successful struggle for tenure at Harvard, but not before taking a position at the University of Chicago. I entered the job market in 1975–76. Berkeley had three openings that year, the result of many years of failed hiring, itself due to deep divisions within the department. The previous year Berkeley had shockingly denied tenure to Jeffrey Paige, winner of the American Sociological Association's best book award for his Marxist-inspired *Agrarian Revolution* (1975). Initially my own application to Berkeley was thrown out – my work was too "ideological."

My job application included a red-baiting letter of "recommendation" from my old benefactor, Edward Shils. He had thought that Chicago professionalism would either straighten me out or cast me out. No such luck. His letter traced my biography from grammar school, where any imagination I may have possessed was snuffed out by cramming in mathematics. Damning with faint praise, he concluded his letter: "Either the security of sectarianism or a juvenile antinomianism seems to have got the better of him. I first noticed the latter in Cambridge. At the time he was an undergraduate and I thought it would pass. Thus far it has not." For such an anti-communist éminence grise as Edward Shils it was especially important to keep Marxism out of the top universities, especially Berkeley, already tainted by a dangerous radicalism.

Rejection by the faculty, however, did not deter Berkeley's graduate students. Led by Erik Wright, still a graduate student at Berkeley but already on his way to Wisconsin, students invited me to visit when I was interviewing at the University of California–Los Angeles. At UCLA the chair had torn up Shils's letter, whereas Berkeley had used it to defame me. As it turned out, my visit to Berkeley became an informal job interview with several sympathetic faculty and students. After I left students mobilized. When the candidates for the urban slot didn't meet expectations, I was moved out of the "comparative" position to become a surrogate urbanist based on my Chicago factory study. Log-rolling ensued and I was offered the job without a formal interview. Had there been a formal interview I have no doubt there would have been enough opposition to veto my candidacy. Needless to say, with today's strict rules regulating recruitment such hiring manipulation would be impossible.

I became a token Marxist assistant professor in the Berkeley department when Marxism and feminism had become major influences among graduate students. If that was not challenging enough, it was made more daunting by being thrown into a den of warring colleagues. Students had largely given up on the faculty. Constituting their own study groups and courses, they were teaching themselves the latest twists and turns of critical theory. The very best could thrive in such a laissez-faire atmosphere, but many were so disenchanted as to never complete their degrees. My first six years at Berkeley were dogged by a mounting conspiracy to deny me tenure. The battle reached its climax with a series of underhand tactics: stacking committees, unsolicited damning letters from prominent sociologists, and the discrediting of my teaching. Fortunately, Robert Bellah, then chair of the department, incensed by the foul play, resolutely went to bat for me and so did the highest committee in the university. The overkill of my enemies backfired.

The skullduggery suggested, at least, that there was something important at stake within the discipline – a new generation with new paradigms was threatening to displace the old. But it was not reducible to a crude struggle for power – although it often felt that way. It took place on a shared terrain of scientific standards. Erik Wright used the latest statistical models to demonstrate that his vision of class was better equipped to understand changing patterns of inequality than the more conventional models of stratification. I tried to show how industrial sociology was simply asking the wrong question and organization theory had the wrong answer. We used the techniques of sociology to present an alternative vision of US society and a different sociology.

As a professional sociologist I took the criticisms of *Manufacturing Consent* to heart. And there were serious criticisms. One of the most abiding attacks came from the guardians of generalizability. How could I possibly make any general claims about capitalism based on a single case study of a single plant in a single corporation? I needed to have conducted a number of such case studies to discover a common pattern. I responded to the criticism in two ways. First, drawing on the philosophy and history of science, I advanced a methodology, "the extended case method," that gives priority to theory, so that a single case study can stimulate the extension of theory (Burawoy 2009). Second, on the basis of my case study of Allis-Chalmers I developed the concept of "production regime," that is, the mode of regulating the relationship between capital and labor within the workplace. This was a theoretical intervention within Marxism, proposing that there is a politics at the point of production as well as at the level of the state. Based on secondary sources I showed how production regimes varied between early and advanced capitalism, within and among different advanced capitalist societies, between advanced capitalism and state socialism, and finally what it looked like in the colonial and postcolonial context (Burawoy 1985). This created a research program that others could advance with their own case studies.

If the first criticism was about *generalization*, the second was about *extension*. My critics questioned the seemingly arbitrary way I extended out from my experiences on the shop floor to forces beyond the plant that were shaping those experiences. Specifically, they questioned the imputation that the hegemonic organization of work was a product of capitalism rather than a system of "industrial relations" typical of progressive industrialization. It required, therefore, that I show that production politics were profoundly different within noncapitalist industry. It seemed to me that the most critical comparison was between advanced capitalism and state socialism – actually existing socialism, or, as I liked to call it, "socialism on earth" as opposed to an imaginary socialism in heaven. While it did point to a distinctive socialist production politics, the material at my disposal on the Soviet order, whether in the Soviet Union or Eastern Europe, was decidedly thin. So during the 1980s I embarked on research into Hungarian factories, again through observant participation, showing the way production politics differed under state socialism, and, indeed, how it contributed to the collapse of state socialism (Burawoy and Lukács 1992). I followed this with a decade of research into the Russian transition from state socialism to capitalism, a transition that had never been seriously imagined within Marxism or sociology. This required me to shift my lens from production to markets, from exploitation to commodification. To frame my arguments I turned to Karl Polanyi's *The Great Transformation* (1944), that was fast becoming a canonical work. The direction of Marxism was shifting once again.

11

Advancing a Research Program

When I arrived in Berkeley, faculty and graduate students alike were puzzled by what seemed to be a combination of opposites: ethnography and Marxism. After all, they said, ethnography, or *participant observation*, concerned itself with micro-processes, social interaction in bounded situations, whereas Marxism concerned itself with macro-processes, large-scale historical transformations. They were irreconcilably opposed. My task, then, was to show just how micro and macro could be joined to each other, how they necessarily feed into each other.

There were reasons for their skepticism. In those days the conventional wisdom about ethnography, at least within sociology, was to be found in Barney Glaser and Anselm Strauss's *The Discovery of Grounded Theory* (1967) – an inductive view of social science that built up theory through constant comparison of observations. It was Chicago sociology's response to the ascendancy of grand theory that sprung from the head of Talcott Parsons rather than from the concrete experiences of real people in social interaction. Ethnography was, therefore, limited to micro-processes, paradigmatically represented by the "dramaturgy" of Erving Goffman or the early Chicago urban studies. The "external" context was bracketed as being beyond the focus of study or simply possessing no meaning.

Coming from Zambia, where the Manchester School had refused the insulation of the field site and pioneered the extended case method (van Velsen 1967), this didn't make sense – the wider context was composed of forces that were shaping face-to-face social interaction. The very meaning of sociology is bound up with linking the micro to the macro, recognizing that the micro is shaped by conditions beyond itself. There were those, such as the distinguished sociologist James Coleman, who, leaning on economics and rational choice theory, pursued the micro-foundations of a macro-sociology. The extended case method, by contrast, called for the study of the macro-foundations of micro-sociology. However, to explore that context ethnographic research required a conception of social science very different from the one that supported grounded theory.

I needed to be schooled in the philosophy of science. Here I was fortunate to learn from Tom Long, an extraordinary graduate student in sociology. Even when he was an undergraduate in Berkeley's philosophy department I attended the summer courses on "critical theory" that he voluntarily organized and led. As part of *his* qualifying examinations, he taught *me* the rudiments of the philosophy of science, the move from the conventional positivist view based on induction, that dominates sociology, to the historical view that pays attention to how science actually works. What I learned from Tom became the basis of an introductory course on methodology required of first-year graduate students. Rather than a rundown of the standard techniques used in sociological research – surveys, participant observation, experimental methods, archival work – my version turned on the question of whether sociology was a science. Drawing on examples of social research, I outlined a sequence of distinct perspectives on the meaning of science: John Stuart Mill's (1888) induction, Karl Popper's (1963) falsificationism, Paul Feyerabend's (1975) anarchism, Michael Polanyi's (1958) personal knowledge, Thomas Kuhn's

(1962) scientific revolutions, and Imre Lakatos's (1978) scientific research programs. In the second half of the course we examined the critiques of sociology as a science, showing how they, too, usually assumed a limited and outdated positivist view of science.

What did this mean for conducting ethnography? Against the discovery of grounded theory, in which theory springs spontaneously from data, the post-positivist theories of science – Kuhn and Lakatos in particular – tell us that one cannot interpret the empirical without some sort of lens, some sort of prior theory that brings order to our observations, allowing us to make sense of what is an infinite manifold. But, as it shines a light on the empirical world, so theory also reveals its own shortcomings, generating expectations that turn out to be false – what we call *anomalies*. Faced with such an empirical challenge, we can either reject the theory or we can hold on to the theory by reconstructing it, maintaining its basic assumptions, but revising it by introducing new "auxiliary hypotheses." In *Manufacturing Consent*, I held on to Marxist assumptions about exploitation but reconstructed the theory of how it works – not through coercion alone but through consent backed up by coercion. Marxist theory also pointed me to the external forces shaping the dynamics on the shop floor. Specifically, markets and states as mediated by the industrial enterprise set the limits – changing limits – on class relations on the shop floor.

I developed this view of the extended case method through teaching a graduate practicum in participant observation. Students were thrown into a field of their choice and had to report on their observations in seminars that met twice a week. They submitted their field notes to me and their classmates, showing how they were grappling with a sociological literature that posed a set of questions to their fieldsite. As they engaged with the people they studied, they simultaneously developed a dialogue between theory and data that ended not in the discovery of theory but its reconstruction.

On two occasions, student papers became the basis of a book. The first, *Ethnography Unbound* (1991), was a collective project organized around studies in the Bay Area, focusing on social movements, education, work, and immigration. This became the occasion for advancing the idea of the extended case method with four components. The first component was to *extend the observer to the participant* – the observer would join participants in their time and space. The idea was not to pretend to be a fly on the wall, but to actually partake in the lives of those they studied. By itself this created multiple dilemmas, especially when the site involved antagonistic actors. Rarely was there a simple solution to these dilemmas, but discussing them collectively made us acutely aware of the challenges in being part of the world we studied.

The second component was to *extend observations over time and space*. Ethnography is not a one-shot event, but a succession of visits that could stretch over months or even years, often requiring the ethnographer to follow their subjects to different places. The idea here is to study the unfolding of social processes, as I did when I followed Zambianization as forced succession within an organization, or the dynamics of the shop floor at Allis. If these first two components are quite typical of participant observation, the third and fourth components are not.

The third component was *the extension of theory*. The extended case method takes the view that theory, understood as a parsimonious summary of the state of collective knowledge in a particular area, is the sine qua non for scientific advances – the extension of theory through the discovery of anomalies. If you start with theory, then a single case can advance that theory – reconstructing it to absorb the anomaly. Grounded theory, by contrast, is not grounded in theory but in the empirical world from which it *induces* empirical regularities, *seemingly* independent of the knowledge accumulated by the scientific community. Grounded theory is actually impossible. There is no way to see the world without a lens, without a cognitive map.

That being the case it's best not to strive for the impossible, but to start from a different premise – the priority of theory.

The extension of theory makes possible a final, fourth extension, the *extension from micro to the macro*, from social interaction to the forces shaping that interaction. Here it is necessary to work with social theory that contains an understanding of the relationship between micro and macro. Grounded theory, resting as it does on induction, cannot go beyond the observations made in the ethnographic field site. Grounded theory may have served its purpose in contesting grand theory, but it has no justification as a scientific method – although it appeals to the empiricist proclivities of US sociology. Sadly, grounded theory leaves theory to the theorist, perpetuating the division it was designed to dissolve.

Ethnography Unbound exemplified the extended case method with ten projects, embedded in divergent theoretical perspectives. As a second collaborative enterprise, *Global Ethnography* (2000) aimed to extend the extended case method to the global arena. I had been made chair of my department, thereby temporarily putting an end to my ethnographic projects. I proposed to the students whose doctoral research I was supervising at the time that we write a book together. They were a brilliant and disparate group, studying different phenomena in different parts of the world. Our task was to forge their studies into a common perspective on globalization. We started, therefore, as a reading group, tackling the most notable theories of globalization associated with such figures as Immanuel Wallerstein, Stuart Hall, Saskia Sassen, David Harvey, Nancy Fraser, Manuel Castells, Anthony Giddens, James Clifford, Arjun Appadurai, Fredric Jameson, and Janet Abu-Lughod. Taking up the loose framing of Stuart Hall, we came up with three approaches to globalization: extranational forces shaping lived experience within nations, transnational connections binding people across national boundaries, and postnational imaginations that informed an emergent global social consciousness. We could ground lofty theories in lived experience but we had greater difficulty working from the lived experience up to the global.

Alongside these ethnography seminars I was developing an alternative research program that extended the theory advanced in *Manufacturing Consent*. I have already pointed to the way I examined changes in production regimes, comparing my own observations and experiences with those of Donald Roy thirty years earlier that led to the contrast between hegemonic and despotic regimes of production. Another serendipitous breakthrough came with the discovery of Miklós Haraszti's riveting book, *A Worker in a Worker's State* (1977). As a political dissident Haraszti had been consigned to work as a machine operator in the Red Star Tractor Factory. He took revenge on his "jailers" with a lurid sociography of life in the socialist factory. As luck would have it, Red Star's machine shop was similar to the one at Allis-Chalmers, with its array of drills, mills, and lathes. But with one striking difference: he worked twice as hard as we did, running two machines at once. This was a dizzying pace, defying the stereotype that workers under state socialism had retained only one right – the right not to work hard. Here was another anomaly, an intriguing puzzle to be explored.

Haraszti's goal was to represent Red Star Tractor Factory as the typical socialist workplace, marked by a despotism driven by piece rates. He did not investigate whether it was, indeed, a typical socialist workplace. That would have entailed recognition of the particular context – time and place – of Red Star as well as his own peripheral vision from within the workplace. It turned out, on further exploration, that Red Star was one of the early factories to be subject to Hungary's New Economic Mechanism of the 1970s that brought market forces to bear on state enterprises. It involved speed-ups and tightening worker discipline. Still, there was always a latent despotism in the state socialist workplace, governed as it was by the collaboration of party, union, and management, each an extension of the state. I called this *bureaucratic despotism* in contrast to the hegemonic regime at Allis, where management had been constrained by the collective contract negotiated with the union and, more broadly, by state regulation of labor relations. In advanced capitalism the state regulates at a distance; it does not have an institutional presence on the shop floor.

One theoretical-conceptual advance immediately called forth another: to distinguish between the bureaucratic despotism at Red Star and the market despotism that Marx had described for nineteenth-century England. I was therefore led to accounts of the nineteenth-century workplace and discovered different despotic regimes – patriarchal and paternalistic. Examining historical accounts from other countries, I showed how the nineteenth-century textile industry exhibited different regimes in Russia and the US, as compared to England. I had to distinguish all of these from the despotic regimes of colonialism – a form of racial despotism – and here I delved into the transitions taking place in the Zambian copper mines, based on my fieldwork there. In every case I not only tried to show how the combination of states and markets created distinctive despotic regimes but also to examine the consequences those regimes had for class formation and the organization of class struggle.

Having shown that states and markets shaped despotic regimes of production, I then had to demonstrate how they shaped different hegemonic regimes under advanced capitalism. The hegemonic regime at Allis-Chalmers exhibited features that were distinctive to the US, as I learned when I began comparing the US with Sweden, Japan, and the UK. Based on studies of factories in these countries, I argued that two factors were crucial: on the one hand, the support states gave to workers when they lost their jobs, and on the other hand, the extent to which the state regulated the relations between capital and labor.

I slowly built up a research program for production regimes, or what I called the *politics of production* (Burawoy 1985), by drawing on secondary accounts that ranged across advanced capitalism, state socialism, and the Global South. But my experiences at Allis-Chalmers had inspired this reconstruction of the Marxist theory of politics and production.

Throughout my time at Berkeley I have had the privilege to work with exceptional students who would push the idea of production politics in different directions by identifying different dimensions of production regimes and how they vary with the labor process, by discovering how regimes differ by economic sector and by national context, and by looking at them from the standpoint of their effects as well as their causes, especially their contribution to working-class mobilization. Let me illustrate these developments with a few of these studies.

Much of the research drew attention to the gendering of production regimes. Ruth Milkman's *Gender at Work* (1987) examines the politics of the gender division of labor in the US electronics and auto industries before, during, and after World War II. She discovers that the distinction between men's work and women's work is rarely contested, but the line between the two moves as a function of the type of industry and managerial interests, rather than because of pressure brought to bear by trade unions or the interests of male workers. Linda Blum's *Between Feminism and Labor* (1991) continues the study of the gender division of labor, comparing the politics of comparable worth that elevates the value of women's work with the politics of affirmative action that promotes women into men's jobs.

Ching Kwan Lee's *Gender and the South China Miracle* (1998) compared production regimes of electronics plants in Hong Kong and Shenzhen: in one there was "familial hegemony" and in the other single women are subjected to "localistic despotism." Ching Kwan attributed their divergence to the wider political economy. Leslie Salzinger's *Genders in Production* (2003) pushed the gendering of production regimes even further through a comparison of four maquiladoras – assembly plants just south of the US/Mexico border. In each plant, management adopted a particular gender strategy: Panoptimex had a patriarchal order sustained through sexualized surveillance, in Anarchomex conflicts around legitimate masculinity continually disrupted managerial control, in Particimex women were incorporated through autonomy and responsibility, and in Andromex all workers were addressed through a putatively "masculine" rhetoric.

Could the idea of production regime be extended from industry to the service sector, and what consequences would ensue? Rachel Sherman studied two luxury hotels where she worked in multiple jobs. *Class Acts* (2007) shows how each hotel is a complex configuration of games in which workers sustain and even create the class identity of guests. Jeff Sallaz's *The Labor of Luck* (2009) compares the regulation of work in casinos in Nevada and Gauteng (South Africa). Despite a strong labor union and government regulation, the production regime in South Africa assumed a despotic form while in Nevada, where the union was nonexistent and government regulation was weak, the production regime was more hegemonic. This puzzling discovery could only be understood by reference to racialized legacies and the wider political context.

Others examined the production politics of state employment. One place to begin was socialist societies. Linda Fuller studied how management, party, and unions shaped workplace politics in Cuba. *Work and Democracy in Socialist Cuba* (1992) shows how decentralized planning allowed for greater worker participation in decisions that affected their daily lives. Starting from his own experiences organizing in the 1980s, Paul Johnston's *Success While Others Fail* (1994) saw the public sector as favoring the building of solidarity between service workers, such as teachers and nurses, and the community they served, while the private sector was governed by a market logic that allowed far less room for such solidarities.

Building on these ideas, Steve Lopez examines union organizing in nursing homes in Pennsylvania: starting at the level of a single senior home, he proceeds to a city-wide campaign and then state-wide organizing. *Reorganizing the Rust Belt* (2004) uncovers distinctive obstacles to unionization at each level: lived experience of prior union campaigns, bureaucratic hierarchies within the union, and employer offensives that take advantage of a permissive legal order. More than two decades later, after the consolidation of neoliberalism, Josh Seim's vivid portrait of the emergency medical technician paints a very different picture. His *Bandage, Sort, and Hustle* (2020) focuses on how the ambulance labor process, embedded in the local state and caught between the hospital and the police, is deployed to govern poverty on the streets.

As the studies of the labor process gave way to studies of the labor movement, greater attention was paid to the *effects* of production regimes. In *Manufacturing Militance* (1994) Gay Seidman traced the 1980s upsurge of working-class struggles in South Africa and Brazil to their similar place in the global order that gave rise to a particular production politics tied to community social movements. Mona Younis's *Liberation and Democratization* (2000) undertakes a historical comparison of the African National Congress (ANC) in South Africa and the Palestinian Liberation Organization, attributing the relative success of the ANC to South African capital's dependence on the colonized. In South Africa, Black workers had accumulated both organizational capacity and structural power, whereas the Israeli state encouraged the importation of labor from elsewhere, expelling Palestinians from the labor market. Palestinians were oppressed but not exploited – they did not have the leverage of South African workers.

Continuing the interest in mobilization, Jennifer Chun's *Organizing at the Margins* (2009) compares the success of organizing among marginalized workers in the US and South Korea, pointing to the importance of a symbolic politics – public shaming of employers – a politics beyond the workplace. Taking us further afield, Ofer Sharone's *Flawed System/Flawed Self* (2013), conceives of unemployment as the hard work of job search. Comparing Israel and the US, he shows how job search is best conceptualized as a labor process game with different dynamics, so that in the US the unemployed blame themselves but in Israel they blame the system. He traces the divergence to the institutional context: the self-help and human resource industry in the US and the ubiquitous private employment agency in Israel.

This embryonic research program was not planned, it emerged spontaneously. Only now do I indulge in a rational reconstruction of what was a largely anarchic process. Graduate students gravitate to particular faculty for different reasons, which often have nothing to do with a common research interest. Many, if not most, of the dissertations I have supervised are beyond my own area of expertise. When common frameworks and questions did emerge, they were not forced upon students but gradually developed through immersion in six to ten years of graduate school. Early on I established a dissertation seminar that has met ever since, every week or two, at which students present their chapters and papers for discussion. Here students learn to discuss one another's work; they are as influenced by one another as they are by myself. I would sometimes present my own work to the group and in one way or another I, too, was influenced by them. Research programs are not necessarily planned; they can just as easily develop spontaneously and imaginatively under multiple influences. Forcing them into a straitjacket only makes them sterile. I suspect that the authors I've identified here would deny that they are part of a research program, just as my fellow workers at Allis denied they were working hard.

Outsiders are often more aware than insiders of an emerging program, labeling students by the reputation of their supervisor or of their department – a reputation that can be derisive as well as flattering. For many years, and indeed to this day, association with me has often been a liability – students would be identified, often unfairly, with my stances on ethnography, public sociology, or Marxism. It continues to cause me much anxiety, especially when it comes to the job market. Inevitably, research programs attract followers but also a lot of critics, and it is easier to criticize vulnerable graduate students than established professors. As long as a research program is confined to a small group within a single department, it is not a disciplinary threat, but when it appeals to followers, especially graduate students, in other departments, then a lively guerrilla warfare unfolds.

In determining the influence of research programs, departmental ranking can have an outsize effect. Had he not been at Harvard, I doubt whether Talcott Parsons would have been able to establish the dominance of structural functionalism. Even within a department, there can be tension between rival research programs competing for dominance. From being a productive tension, competition can tip over into something quite destructive. With its multiplicity of research programs rather than one single dominant research program, combat within US sociology is perhaps less intense and more institutionalized, channeled into different journals, departments, or sections of the American Sociological Association.

When competition moves to the global level it inevitably favors research programs emerging from countries with the deepest research infrastructure. Research programs emanating from the US can hide their provinciality behind bogus claims to universalism, propped up by status and funding. In recent decades the supremacy of US sociology – and to a lesser extent, European sociology – has galvanized transnational opposition. Such collaborations across the Global South have their own originality, but they too may be limited, to the largest countries and even to cosmopolitan intellectuals within them. Such is the nature of Northern academia that leading Southern opponents of

Western thought may find themselves absorbed, co-opted, and celebrated in the metropolis.

Given the hierarchy of global knowledge production, scholars from the South are often lured away by tempting offers from universities in the North, even as they maintain one foot in their home countries. They become authoritative representatives of perspectives on the South within Northern academia. But there are also many who refuse the temptations of the North, and remain embedded in universities and institutes in the South. They often undertake dangerous projects, putting their own lives at stake, developing research programs in collaboration with oppressed communities, generating new visions of what sociology might be and what sociology can prefigure.

12

Painting Socialism

Eyes were riveted to the reports of the momentous strike that had broken out in the Lenin Shipyards in Gdansk, Poland on August 14, 1980. A burgeoning underground movement of intellectuals and workers, organized against the party-state, had been developing for some years. It suddenly burst into the open. Long-time labor activist Lech Wałęsa scaled the fence into the shipyards to lead the public negotiations with the government. Since the strikers wouldn't go to Warsaw, so serious was this threat that the Deputy Prime Minister came to the strikers. He capitulated to the demands of the workers in the hope that the strike would be snuffed out and the strike leaders could then be repressed. That's how it had happened in the past, but not this time. The strikers held firm and their actions spread across the shipyards and into other industries. *Solidarność* quickly became a class-wide national movement that sought to build an autonomous civil society under working-class leadership, but without attacking the state directly. This was both a pragmatic decision for fear of courting a military intervention by the USSR, as had happened in Budapest in 1956 and Prague in 1968, and a political decision based on the belief that any engagement with the state would compromise the movement. As Jadwiga Staniszkis (1984) wrote, this Polish revolution was a "self-limiting revolution."

I prepared to go to Poland, reading everything I could, learning Polish and securing leave. But academic life has its own rhythm that bears little relation to the world beyond. By the time I was ready to go, General Jaruzelski had declared martial law (December 13, 1981), and *Solidarność* went underground. My chance to study the first societal-wide working-class revolt in history had evaporated, but my interest in Eastern Europe was irreversible. It was then that I had the good fortune to meet the dissident Hungarian sociologist Iván Szelényi, author with George Konrád of *The Intellectuals on the Road to Class Power* – one of the great theoretical treatises on state socialism, which would profoundly shape my own understanding. Iván had recently been recruited to the University of Wisconsin–Madison, where I was also headed in the expectation that my career at Berkeley was about to be terminated with the denial of tenure.

Hearing of my interest in Eastern Europe, Iván sponta-neously invited me to join him and his wife in their return to Hungary. He had been in exile in Australia since 1976. The summer of 1982 would be his first homecoming. I gratefully and enthusiastically accepted. This first visit behind the "iron curtain" proved to be a most exhilarating experience – ten days that shook my life. In Hungary I discovered a thriving socialism and, with it, a thriving sociology. Despite our opposed views of Marxism, I had much in common with a lively cohort of young sociologists interested in labor markets and work organization, and in the famous Hungarian economic reforms.

Polish Solidarity presented a major anomaly to a Marxist understanding of the world: the revolutionary movement of the working class was supposed to happen under capitalism, not state socialism. History throws up lots of surprises for Marxism and this was one I was deter-mined to pursue. With Poland blocked off as a research site, and with the help of Iván and his colleagues, I set about planning fieldwork in Hungary. The puzzle became more complicated. If before the question was "why did the first working-class revolution take place in Eastern Europe?" now it had an additional level, why did it take place in Poland and not in Hungary, especially given the dramatic, albeit short-lived, 1956 revolt in Hungary? I naturally turned to the politics of production and asked two questions: first, what was the distinctive feature of socialist production and second, what was the class consciousness of its workers.

I needed to enter the hidden abode of the socialist workplace – one of the most protected sites of state socialism, off limits to almost any researcher, let alone a sociologist from the US. In 1983 I took off for Hungary for six months, ready to take intensive language lessons and hoping to find work in some factory. As it turned out, learning Hungarian proved to be far harder than acquiring work, which – with the help of friends – I found in a champagne factory on a collective farm and in a small textile shop on an agricultural cooperative. Getting a job in Hungary's industrial heartland proved to be more challenging. It was only through the ingenuity of fellow Hungarian sociologist János Lukács that I was able to land a job the following summer of 1984 in a machine shop in Eger's Csepel Auto factory, producing gearboxes for the famous Ikarus buses.

The technology was the same as I had operated at Allis, and Haraszti had operated at Red Star. We were all paid on a piece rate system. At Csepel Auto, however, we did not work at Haraszti's level of intensity. When I arrived in 1984 the early experiments in economic reform had passed and Red Star had actually disappeared. I became focused on comparing my experiences at Csepel Auto with Allis-Chalmers. We were running similar machines and paid on a piece rate system, but there were some crucial differences.

At Csepel *employment* was guaranteed but not *earnings*, whereas the reverse held at Allis – earning guarantees without employment security. At Csepel we received a pay that corresponded to how much we produced as individuals. If a machine broke down or there was a shortage of materials, our wages suffered. At Allis our wages might also suffer, but there was an acceptable minimum below which wages did not fall. The difference in the piece rate system explained how Haraszti found himself running two machines at once – at Red Star that was the norm required for a living wage. If managers at Allis had cut the piece rates in two – doubled the work intensity – we would simply have worked to rule and received the minimum wage.

Most surprising, however, was that production at Csepel seemed more organized than at Allis, refuting conventional wisdom that capitalist firms were more efficient than socialist firms. As a mark of inefficiency, unfinished engines piled up in the aisles at Allis – the sort of thing you'd expect in a stereotypical socialist factory, but this did not happen at Csepel. More generally, at Csepel there was a more flexible work organization, an adaptation to the shortage economy – shortages of materials and personnel, unreliable machinery and so forth – that characterized the socialist economy just as surpluses and lay-offs characterize the capitalist economy. We see how the different economies – market versus administered – led to different conditions of production and different modes of regulation – that is, different regimes of production: hegemonic versus bureaucratic.

But this didn't explain why workers were more likely to engage in revolutionary action under state socialism than under advanced capitalism. To explore this question I investigated the conditions at the heart of the socialist working class – in the Lenin Steel Works (LKM), at that time the biggest steel complex in Hungary. For me to enter the Lenin Steel Works was nothing short of a miracle – once again made possible by the elaborate networking and negotiation of my colleague and collaborator, János Lukács.

Concerned to impress me but also to keep an eye on me, the managers at Lenin Steel Works installed me at the heart of production – tending the great 80-ton converter where molten pig iron is turned into steel under high-pressure oxygen at a temperature of 1,700 degrees centigrade. I was a member of the October Revolution Socialist Brigade – a brigade of furnace men who shoveled in the alloys and tested the quality of the steel. Although this job was more dangerous than any of my previous ones – an overhead crane could tip and drop molten steel on my head and I would be burnt alive – I, at least, could not easily endanger the lives of others. It was a relief to be working in the same brigade week in week out, even though I never got used to the shift rotation every three days.

The Combined Steel Works – as it was called – had been equipped with the latest technologies from Sweden, Japan, and Austria, but they did not always work well together. Here was another reason why the immediate labor process required flexible organization: to adapt to the misaligned technologies. Management, however, would not give up its authority, continually appropriating control from the shop floor, often with disastrous results.

During the period 1985–88, I worked at LKM for about a year altogether, exploring not just the organization of work but the consciousness of workers. Unlike capitalism, where exploitation was invisible to workers, managers, and capitalists alike, state socialism made it visible for all to see, orchestrated through the combined agency of management, trade union, and party, all extensions of the state at the point of production. The party, supported by management and trade union, organized rituals of collective affirmation. On one such occasion they collectively condemned our interim report that emphasized the key role of the shop floor operators and the problematic intervention of management. We were told to do the research again and we happily complied, only to come up with the same conclusions.

One of my favorite moments emerged during an extra, unpaid "communist" (Saturday) shift to clean up the steel mill in preparation for the visit of the Prime Minister.

We were ordered to paint the "slag drawer" in a bright yellow and green. This struck us as a rather absurd task, given the metallic dust that settled everywhere. Orders are orders, but I could only find a black paintbrush. So I started to paint our shovels – the most important equipment of the furnace man – black. The supervisor came roaring over, asking me what the hell I was doing. Mustering up as much innocence as I could, I declared that I was building socialism. My fellow workers from the October Revolution Socialist Brigade cracked up, but the supervisor was furious. Then the brigade jokester – called ET because years of drinking made him look like ET, his skin bulging and sagging under his eyes – piped up, "Misi, Misi. You are not *building* socialism, you are *painting* socialism, and *black* at that."

"Painting socialism" was a metaphor for the party-state declaring socialism to be just, egalitarian, and efficient when workers experienced the opposite – injustice, inequality, and inefficiency. Workers held the party-state accountable for failing to live up to its own ideology. In turning the values of socialism against actually existing socialism, workers were, despite themselves, announcing a commitment to socialism and its goals. Or so I thought. When socialism dissolved in 1989 I was expecting – wishful thinking as it turned out – workers to mobilize for an alternative democratic socialism. There were small groups who tried to resuscitate the worker councils of 1956, but for the most part workers had given up on socialism, thinking that only capitalism could solve the irrationalities of the shortage economy, not realizing that capitalism comes with its own irrationalities.

Throughout my time in Hungary, I was bent on explaining why you might get a working-class movement like *Solidarność* in state socialism but not in advanced capitalism. Here my explanation followed a Marxist analysis of the relationship between work organization (relations in production) and the system of planning (relations of production). Under state socialism, the central appropriation and redistribution of surplus led to a shortage economy and, thus, requiring relative autonomy in the workplace. However, this same *bureaucratic regime* also required ideological justification, a process of *legitimation* that became the mainspring of the critique of state socialism – a critique that could spill over into collective organization, and thereby invite political repression. Production under advanced capitalism does not require legitimation because exploitation is hidden and the hegemonic regime of production organizes consent to the rule of management without direct intervention of the state. Capitalism is a peculiar mode of production in that the economy operates with relative autonomy from the external realm of politics. Legitimacy is necessary not to reproduce the relations of production but to forestall or contain mobilized challenges to the social order that are actually few and far between.

But why did the Solidarity Movement appear in Poland and not in Hungary? In both places exploitation was transparent, requiring legitimation that led to the questioning of socialism on its own terms. In both economies, shortages called forth autonomous initiative from workers. So where did the difference lie? Here I was compelled to look beyond the workplace to understand the conditions under which class consciousness forged in production gave rise to class formation, how class *in* itself became a class *for* itself. In Poland there was an embryonic civil society, protected by the Roman Catholic Church, that allowed workers to develop a collective dissenting voice, whereas Hungary's embryonic civil society was dominated by a market economy, or what was called a *second economy*, through which workers advanced their individual interests through second jobs and cooperatives. They became socialist entrepreneurs rather than an organized political force. In this way I tried to explain the instability of state socialism, and why opposition to state socialism might take the form of a social movement in Poland rather than Hungary.

My research led me to criticism of both social science and Marxism. Social scientists, economists, political scientists, and sociologists, were guilty of a false comparison – comparing an idealized version of capitalism with the dysfunctional realities of state socialism. American sociology had condemned "communism's" undemocratic ways, its inefficiencies and mendacities, on the implicit and unexamined assumption that advanced capitalism is democratic, efficient, and transparent. If the latter deviated from the ideal, this was of minor importance, easily ironed out. Postwar sociology had become an anti-communist crusade that celebrated the US as the promised land and condemned the Soviet Union and China as totalitarian enemies. My intention, and that of others, was to rectify the balance by comparing like with like – production in capitalism with production under socialism. Furthermore, it was important to see how ideology played a different role in the two systems and, above all, not to mistake ideology for sociology.

Marxism was guilty of the reverse sin. *Soviet* Marxism was a crude ideology designed to create an illusory view of state socialism by obscuring its class character and its irrationalities while *Western* Marxism too easily dismissed the Soviet Union and its satellites as a form of statism (or capitalism) unrelated to socialism. Western Marxists thereby avoided dealing with the realities of state socialism; instead they postulated a utopian *idealization* of socialism against the dystopian *realities* of capitalism. I opposed this creation of an unexplicated socialist utopia with which to condemn capitalism, and instead committed myself to exploring actually existing socialism as a sometimes monstrous and always unsatisfactory form of society, riddled with its own contradictions. To its detriment, Marxism rarely probed this extraordinary attempt to build socialism on earth, preferring to leave it in heaven. However, to be a science is to confront and deal with inconvenient truths.

13

The Great Involution

In 1989 Hungary exited from communism, forging a double transition from the party-state to an open liberal democracy and from state socialism to capitalism. In the first half of 1990 I was on sabbatical in Hungary, following my colleague János Lukács who had become an ardent advocate of ESOPs (Employee Stock Ownership Plans) as a strategy of privatization – transforming public enterprises into worker-owned enterprises. He was busy applying the results of our research: that the state socialist economy had depended on the ingenuity of shop floor workers to adapt to endemic shortages. Drawing on that legacy, he argued that workers were often better placed to manage their workplace than managers themselves and, therefore, they should own and control their own enterprises.

As a consultant on worker participation, János took me to visit various plants, including the famous Herend Porcelain Factory that exported its products the world over. Herend had become a showcase for the post-communist transition to worker-owned factories. I was less enthusiastic about this proxy-socialism, a distraction from Hungary's dismal descent into capitalism. I was disappointed that the socialist project had been abandoned so abruptly, so enthusiastically. So I turned my attention to the USSR, the still-standing state socialist Behemoth.

As fate would have it, amid the mail my friend Bob Freeland forwarded from Berkeley was a message from Moscow, inviting me to participate in a ten-day "summer school" for industrial sociologists. It was to take place in the second half of May on a boat going down the Volga. I had been to the Soviet Union on five previous occasions, either for conferences or for Erik Wright's collaboration with Soviet sociologists to develop a joint US–USSR social survey. I had grown wary of these expeditions, as there was so little serious engagement with our counterparts – ritualized culture contact with little substance. Still, disillusioned with what I was seeing around me in Hungary, curious what was going on in Russia, and tempted by a trip on the Volga, I accepted the invitation. It was another ten days that shook my life!

Nina Andreenkova, head of the industrial sociology unit at the Soviet Academy of Sciences, had invited four of us from the US to lecture to some 170 "plant sociologists." In reality they were employed in personnel management or human resources, and drawn from enterprises across the Soviet Union. The participants were sponsored by their enterprises to attend a paid "working holiday" (*kommandirovka*) – a wonderful Soviet invention – which meant lectures in the morning, tourism along the river in the afternoon, drinking and partying under the starlit sky in the evening. Now that was real communism! I didn't speak any Russian, but Nina had brought along several interpreters both for the lectures and the informal festivities, and two of my colleagues from the US spoke Russian.

This was the summer of 1990 – wild and uncertain times in the Soviet Union, the climax of Gorbachev's *glasnost* (openness), *perestroika* (reconstruction), and *uskoreniye* (acceleration). While we were traveling down the Volga on a boat, appropriately named the *Gogol*, the newly established Russian parliament was in its first raucous session, promoting Yeltsin and Russian independence. As I learned from my companions, factories were also experiencing tumultuous times, especially in the coal industry, where miners were launching unprecedented challenges to the party-state.

One evening I let it be known that my father was born in Dniepropetrovsk, a huge industrial center in the Ukraine. I was immediately surrounded by employees of enterprises in the area. This is when trouble began. Dniepropetrovsk was a closed city, a home to the Soviet nuclear and space industry where some of my companions worked. And this was still the Soviet Union, so there were party informants on board, taking note of who was talking to whom. Nina Andreenkova had taken a huge risk in letting foreigners loose among all these enterprise sociologists. At Gorky, the police came on board and started cross-examining some of our Soviet companions, a cross-examination that would follow them back home. As I would learn, the KGB and its successor the FSB would rarely interrogate me; rather, they would question the people with whom I worked. They were concerned with controlling their own population, and not the exploits of a foreigner who was simply the bait.

Despite this rather unpleasant turn of events, the trip proved to be another turning point for me. It was on the *Gogol* that I met my future collaborators, Kathryn Hendley, a political science graduate student at Berkeley, and Pavel Krotov, a sociologist from Syktyvkar, the capital of the Komi Republic in Northern Russia. I had often dreamt of conducting research in the Soviet Union, but never thought it would be feasible. But now that things were opening up anything was possible. I returned in January 1991. By August, Yeltsin was standing defiantly on the tank, repelling the attempted coup; by the end of the year the Soviet Union was no more, dissolving before my eyes, disappearing with barely a whimper. At least, this time, I was not too late.

My Soviet expedition began in a historic Moscow rubber factory, Kauchuk, at the beginning of 1991 (Burawoy and Hendley 1992) – entry facilitated by the gift of two portable computers to the trade union. Kathie Hendley was the key networker, interpreter, and organizer. The enterprise had become the site of a civil war, a public feud between, on the one side, the "young Turks," mainly engineers, who supported the creation of a market economy and the exodus of Russia from the Soviet Union, and, on the other side, the old guard that included the enterprise president and the chief engineer, who doggedly defended the planned economy and the integrity of the Soviet Union. Kauchuk struggled to survive in that winter of 1991, as material shortages paralyzed day-to-day production. But management was able to exploit the collapsing central planning apparatus. They accumulated wealth by spinning off privatized cooperatives that bled the company of its supplies. I'd seen all this before in Hungary at the Lenin Steel Works, as managers privatized the lucrative part of the enterprise and, for a short period, made a killing in the emerging markets.

After three months in Moscow I decamped to Northern Russia, to the Republic of Komi. This was a region well-endowed with natural resources – coal, oil, and gas as well as vast swaths of forest that formed the basis of its timber industry. It had been home to a string of famous labor camps. At the heart of the complex was the very northerly mining city of Vorkuta. Life in such camps has been well described by Alexander Solzhenitsyn in *One Day in the Life of Ivan Denisovich*. While Pavel and I did spend time in Vorkuta, the labor camps had long since disappeared, finally closed in 1962.

I began the exploration of Soviet production in Syktyvkar, the capital of Komi, a city with a population of some 230,000. That was where Pavel lived with his mother in a run-down wooden tenement. Unlike so many Soviet sociologists who thought the survey was the only instrument of investigation and frowned upon anything like ethnography, Pavel was a man of the people, born to be an ethnographer. We got to know the leader of the trade union federation, who would later become a major political player in Komi as Governor of the Republic.

Through him I would get a job in Syktyvkar's youthful
furniture factory that specialized in the production of
wall systems – the combination of shelves and cabinets
that adorned every Soviet apartment. Once again I was
assigned to drill holes, only this time in wood – here
perhaps it was more appropriate, as my Russian surname
seemed to connote an artisan in drilling holes (Burawoy
and Krotov 1992).

Fellow workers had difficulty comprehending what I
was doing there. An American professor drilling holes in
a Soviet factory had to be some sort of spy. It turned out
that they were much more concerned about my being a spy
for management than for the CIA. What I didn't realize
at the time was that the shop floor supervisor used me to
discipline her workers. She regularly intoned, "There's an
American here, you had better turn up to work on time."
Eventually, my patience paid off and I was invited to play
dominoes in our many hours of downtime waiting for
materials to arrive.

As the planned economy dissolved in 1991, Northern
Furniture was able to barter its monopoly of the production
of wall systems into all sorts of desirable and scarce
supplies for its workers – from alcohol to shoes, from meat
and sugar to places in holiday homes in the South. This
was Northern Furniture's short honeymoon period, able to
exploit its monopoly position in the transitional economy.
When I returned the following year, after the dissolution
of the Soviet Union, the factory was already in dire straits
and on the way to bankruptcy, along with so much of the
economy – few had the resources to buy wall systems and
those who did preferred higher quality imports.

The transition to the market decimated the industrial economy as enterprise after enterprise closed down.
Together with a small collective of Syktyvkar sociologists,
my research took a new turn – how families survived this
economic catastrophe. It involved in-depth interviewing
of selected employees and their families. To discover their
complex strategies of survival was by no means easy, as

this involved a tacit knowledge of household strategies that informants had difficulty articulating. Only a talented local sociologist, Tatyana Lytkina – immersing herself in their worlds, following their day-to-day decisions through gentle but perpetual interrogation – could ever comprehend how families made out in those precarious conditions. Given that existence in the Soviet era had required flexible adaptation to a shortage economy, families could draw on inherited psychological and social resources to face the inexorable postindustrial decline. It was a gendered response, however, in which working-class men, accustomed to security of employment, had far greater difficulty adapting than women, who had always borne the greater responsibility for family welfare. Now they supported their households through chains of mutual help and barter, through securing benefits from the state, through self-employment and creating small businesses, and through growing their own food on small intensively cultivated plots of land.

The bewildering transition from security to precarity tested the limits of endurance. Most were left in poverty while a few made a killing – those that controlled the market, namely bankers and mafia groups and those who positioned themselves to appropriate the proceeds of privatization. Pavel and I tried to study bankers, but it was far more difficult than studying factories – the production process was invisible, even to bank employees. You could study a bank for months but never know anything about the financial machinations that were keeping it afloat. Fortunately, we failed to plumb the depths of financial capital. I say "fortunately" because, at that time in the 1990s, bankers were being regularly shot or imprisoned. Instead, we turned to housing construction – how it survived in what had become a barter economy. Housing was at the center of the economy but it was also at the center of everyone's life. There was new housing, but it was largely built for the nouveau riche who had benefited financially from the transition. We developed an account of social mobility between housing classes and the strategies families deployed to maintain a roof over their heads.

Despite their ingenuity, the market transition was a disaster for the majority of the population. In the eyes of those who expected a bonanza – such as the miners of Vorkuta – the problem was not the hallowed market but the legacy of communism. The disaster of transition demonstrated that 70 years of communism had created such an infertile soil that no effective market could grow. Indeed, this was the theory that led some economists to propose shock therapy: destroy everything in a revolutionary break with the past. Other economists saw this as foolishness – you can't create something out of nothing; you need to build new institutions in an evolutionary transition. The reality was neither revolution nor evolution but what we called "involution" – a market that was destroying rather than advancing the forces of production.

The expansion of the market led to a "primitive disaccumulation" – the reverse of the process Marx had depicted as the genesis of capitalism – that took place at the cost of economic development. Entrepreneurs were more interested in immediate gains from asset stripping than in the long-term profit from building new enterprises or renovating old ones. As markets expanded, a new class gorged itself on Soviet enterprises. Time horizons shrank as the state was enfeebled. This was all quite different from the market transition in China, where the market was incubated under the direction of the party-state. In Russia the dominant strategy was to ruthlessly destroy everything connected to communism. The past was viewed as a radical impediment to the future. Russia witnessed what we might call a Bolshevik transition to capitalism, which, in many ways, was more disastrous, if less violent in terms of human lives and economic cost, than the original transition to communism.

Marxism could offer an analysis of the *collapse of state socialism* in terms of the suffocation of the productive forces by the relations of production, and could even offer an understanding of class struggles, such as the strike wave led by coal miners in 1989 and then again in 1991, that proved to be the dynamite that brought the Soviet system to its knees. But Marxism as theory had a far more difficult time grasping the *genesis of a post-Soviet capitalism*. The hidden secret of the emerging order lay not in the labor process but in the realm of exchange that was systematically corroding production (Burawoy and Krotov 1993).

Like others, I turned to Karl Polanyi's *The Great Transformation* (1944) that examined the destructive consequences of unregulated markets. This extraordinary book, which has become a canonical work in sociology, shows how the industrial revolution in nineteenth-century England depended on a state-supervised market – "Laissez-fare was planned; planning was not." For the transition from state socialism the lesson was clear – there is no simple market road to market capitalism. Further, as Polanyi argued, once unleashed, markets so threatened society as to give rise to reactive counter-movements that could be worse than the danger they were supposed to avert. In the twentieth century the turn against the market during the Depression could take the form of state-sponsored social democracy but it could also take an authoritarian road – fascism and Stalinism.

I turned to Polanyi's concept of "fictitious commodity" to shed light on what was happening in Russia. A "fictitious commodity" is a force of production that when commodified – that is, reduced to its exchange value – loses its use value. Polanyi focused on three fictitious commodities: land, labor, and money. When labor power is commodified without protection, unregulated exploitation causes wages to fall below the cost of subsistence. When land is commodified, again without any restraint, this destroys the conditions necessary to support humanity, whether through ascending rent in the inner cities of advanced capitalism or the expropriation of peasantries in the Global South or the abuse of land by agribusiness. Finally, when money is commodified so that it becomes the object of speculation, such as in the bizarre financial instruments created from debt, it can no longer act as a reliable medium of exchange, and businesses go out of business.

In post-Soviet Russia all three – land, labor, and money – were suddenly thrown into an unregulated market: labor had no protection and did not receive a living wage even when it was so lucky as to find employment; land was plundered at will and agriculture was driven back to subsistence; money (the ruble) was subject to speculation in a dramatic inflationary spiral, so that the economy turned to barter, prompting the development of local currencies. Our research in Komi revealed each of these processes, but especially the commodification of labor and money. Instead of a "great transformation" Russia underwent a "great involution." Only after eight years of unprecedented economic decline did the Putin revolution bring back some semblance of order and regulation. This was a countermovement of sorts, and, moreover, one Polanyi might anticipate – the rise of an authoritarian regime.

After the great expectations and indeterminacy of the last years of the Soviet regime and the excitement of the early 1990s, Russia had skidded down a steep slope into poverty and decline. I had begun the exploration of "socialism on earth" in Hungary, asking why Solidarity had occurred in Eastern Europe and why in Poland rather than Hungary. I found the answer to lie in the peculiar autonomy of workers on the shop floor and the way state socialism generated its antithesis, a working class that called for a democratic socialism, demanding the party-state realize its promises. Such voices could be heard as state socialism disintegrated at the end of the 1980s, but they were far fainter than the call for the abandonment of socialism altogether as a failed experiment. If I was wrong about the possibilities of democratic socialism, I was right about the capitalist dystopia that would befall them on the edge of Europe. And I was right that they would look back on state socialism as a "radiant past" when there had been security and progress.

The story was repeated in Russia. The working class, but particularly the miners, had been the dynamite to bring down the old order, but they were the first to be sacrificed in the new order, as mines closed down one by one. They had imagined they would control their own mines and their proceeds, but they neglected to consider the broader forces that would make nonsense of their dreams – a utopia without anti-utopia. Komi had been a network of labor camps within the gulag, and now it had become a network of declining communities within capitalism, from captivity without freedom to captivity without security. People fled if they could, but most could not.

I had followed the great involution as it spread through northern Russia. With Polanyi as my compass, I looked for lineaments of a countermovement to the market but discovered only a new authoritarianism. Helpless and without an audience – either among academics or publics or policy makers – I had backed myself onto the edge of the world. Although I saw Russia as the leading edge of a global descent into a neoliberal dystopia, I couldn't connect the dots to the rest of the world. I was too caught up in the distressing peculiarities of the Russian transition, and the loss of any utopian vision. The darkness of the moment outweighed any light of a better future. How was I to recover my faith in sociology? For sociology without utopian imagination is not just blind but empty. The answer came from where I least expected it.

Part Six
Real Utopias

It was some time in 1997 that I received a call from Teresa Sullivan, then Secretary of the American Sociological Association (ASA), more recently President of the University of Virginia (2010–18) where she valiantly defended the university against corporatization. We had been graduate students together in Chicago. "Michael," she said, "it's time you did something for the ASA. I want you to stand for the Publications Committee." She was right. I had done nothing for the ASA. In my mind the ASA represented the dominance of the more conservative elements in US sociology, the very elements against which I had been struggling. Even though I had been at Berkeley for twenty years and was chair of my department, my professionalism was skin deep. Or so I thought. She said, "I just want you to stand; it doesn't mean you'll be elected." Not thinking it was likely that I would be elected, I agreed. Much to my consternation I was elected. A new world opened up before me.

In that first year, the Publications Committee received a handful of submissions for new editors of the association's top professional journal – the *American Sociological Review*. Our role was to evaluate and rank the submissions. After careful study of all the submissions and much discussion we all agreed to put forward two especially enterprising proposals that we thought would give new energy and direction to the journal. Our top choice was a team led by an African American who would have given the journal a new lease of life. Our proposal went to Council, the top legislative body in the ASA, which conventionally rubber-stamps the decisions of the Publications Committee. In this case, however, Council voted to reject both nominations and instead selected another editorial team not even in our top three. We on the Publications Committee were aghast. It confirmed my worst suspicions of professionalism.

We protested without effect – the President said Council was within its rights to overturn a decision of the committee. That was correct, but then why have a Publications Committee? We wanted to protest publicly but our hands were tied by a confidentiality rule – breaking that rule could embarrass those who had been chosen by the Publications Committee and discredit the editors chosen by Council. From our point of view there was a clash of principles – the formal rights of Council against our accountability to the membership we were elected to serve. Already fed up, I inclined toward the latter. I publicly resigned in the summer of 1999 with a letter that explained what had happened and the issues at stake, but mentioning no names. The President accepted my resignation but, he said, in making it public I was in clear violation of the ASA Code of Ethics, and he would charge me with misconduct before the ethics committee. He had declared war, so I circulated his letter to all and sundry. These are the struggles within the professional community: seemingly petty and trivial from the outside, real and significant from the inside.

In standing my ground I had no idea I was tapping into resentment that had been welling up for some time – the membership latched onto the conflict to protest the arrogance of Council. The high-handed action of the President – he could have consulted with the Publications Committee, he could have asked us to reconsider our decision, he could have negotiated a path forward

– crystallized mounting opposition that reached a climax in a massively packed business meeting at the annual meeting of the ASA, when the President and members of Council were roundly condemned. Vindicated but no longer a member of the Publications Committee, I was asked by the nominations committee to stand for Council, which I did, and two years later in 2002 for President, which I also did – in each case winning. This was a very rapid and totally unexpected ascent up the professional hierarchy. Despite my reluctance, fate decreed that I change my attitude.

This entry into the world of professional sociology coincided with a growing disillusionment with my own research. I had begun to wonder what I was doing in the Arctic, witnessing Russia's unregulated descent into merchant capitalism. Here was an opportunity to turn my gaze back on sociology – what did it all mean? The election also coincided with the end of an eight-year stint as department chair that I shared with my close friend and colleague, Peter Evans. As I explained in Chapter 2, throughout that time I had already been promoting the idea of public sociology that, I believed, distinguished Berkeley sociology. Now I had a chance to take this idea into the heart of professional sociology – a return to my naïve vision of sociology cultivated in my Zambian research, but now with thirty years of experience of teaching, research, and administration.

So I became an evangelist for public sociology, arguing that not only did the world need public sociology, but in order to flourish the discipline also needed public engagement. I was not the first to make public sociology central to a campaign. Herb Gans had done it before me when he had been President of the ASA in 1988. But he was less a preacher and more a practitioner, having written a great deal about journalism as well as being immersed in debates over the causes and alleviation of poverty. Where he was looking outwards, I was looking inwards at the composition of our discipline. I placed public sociology in relation to professional, policy, and critical sociologies, and behind that I was asking two fundamental questions: Knowledge for whom? Knowledge for what? (Burawoy 2005). This would lead to more than a decade of ferocious debates, countless articles and symposia, edited collections – all effectively raising the question of what we were up to as sociologists. My national campaign culminated in the ASA's annual meeting of 2004 in San Francisco that broke all attendance records. It was a good time to be advocating for public sociology – the ASA membership had passed motions against the Bush administration's initiation of the Iraq War and against moves to outlaw same-sex marriage.

As ASA President I was using what power I had to set the terms of a debate about the meaning of sociology and, thereby, supporting many who had been marginalized or ignored by the dominant professionalism. I was attacked from every side – professional sociologists attacked public sociology as a cover for my Marxism, policy sociologists attacked me for politicizing the discipline and undermining its scientific credentials, public sociologists attacked me for giving too much credence to professional sociology, critical sociologists attacked me for refusing to endow public sociology with a singular normative stance. But the attacks only gave vitality to the question of public sociology.

During this period, I began visiting South Africa on a regular basis. My friend Eddie Webster, leading labor sociologist in South Africa, director of SWOP (then the Sociology of Work Unit, now the Society, Work and Politics Institute) persuaded me that it was time to give up my Russian research and return to South Africa. So I did. In 2000 Eddie invited me to be an advisor on a Deep Mining Project, investigating the feasibility of gold mining 5 kilometers underground. So began regular visits to South Africa almost every year for the next fifteen years, working with PhD students and faculty tied to SWOP, giving lectures in different departments across South Africa, and

attending conferences. I did not attempt any research of
my own, but focused on trying to understand the practice
of sociology in South Africa, in particular how SWOP
was so successful in engaging with diverse publics through
research, seminars, and their famous breakfasts, attended
by politicians, government officials, unions, and the wider
public.

On one of these trips to South Africa Peter Alexander,
later Kate Alexander, from the University of Johannesburg
invited me to work with his MA students on their
collective research. There on an island in the Vaal River
I met Sujata Patel, who was also invited to work with
the students. It proved to be the beginning of a professional relationship that drew me into the International
Sociological Association (ISA) as well as a succession of
visits to India. Sujata was then ISA Vice-President for
National Associations, and she encouraged me to stand
as her successor. I became Vice-President 2006–10 and
was then elected President, 2010–14. I was becoming the
archetypical professional!

Those eight years gave me a platform to discuss public
sociology in very different places, forcing me to consider
the production and reception of sociology across the globe.
During those years I also taught two (video-recorded)
courses with Laleh Behbehanian – Global Sociology Live!
and Public Sociology Live! – involving Skype-orchestrated
discussions with some of the most inspiring public
sociologists from all over the world. In a parallel venture,
I began *Global Dialogue*, designed to foster international
debate and discussion of contemporary issues through a
sociological lens. It began as a newsletter in three languages
and ended as a colorful quarterly magazine in seventeen
languages, powered and translated by teams of young
sociologists from many different countries. It continues to
this day under the direction of Brigitte Aulenbacher, Klaus
Dörre, and their young colleagues.

Coming to terms with "global sociology" entailed understanding the global field of knowledge production and

consumption, its patterns of domination and exclusion. It meant studying the crises of the university, attempting to situate those crises in a theory of capitalism. Public sociology, in particular, lies suspended between two intersecting fields. On the one hand, it battles for expression within an external field shaped by the forces of capitalism – forces that simultaneously inspire the need for but also circumscribe the possibility of sociological engagement. On the other hand, public sociology is produced within an academic field that is itself shaped by the same capitalism. We need to locate public sociology both in relation to a theory of capitalism and then a theory of the university. That is my task for this last part of the book.

We have already engaged Karl Polanyi's ideas in their application to the Russian transition to capitalism; its pathological form captures key features of the contemporary order – the confluence of precarious labor, a devastated environment, and the corrosive effect of finance capital. Russia also led the way in privatizing the production of knowledge, wrecking its public universities in the process. While I had seen few signs of collective struggles against unregulated capitalism in Russia, my Presidency of the ISA coincided with a wave of social movements that spread across the globe – the new movements of the Arab Spring, Occupy, and Indignados energized older movements of peasants, labor, women, and environmental justice. If anything united these movements, it was not their opposition to economic exploitation in production but to the destructive commodification of what I call third-wave marketization – the subject of the first chapter that follows.

Public sociology cannot ignore third-wave marketization and the devastation it has brought to life on earth and will continue to bring to life on earth if it is not drastically reversed. Public sociology has a special role to play in contesting third-wave marketization. I follow Erik Wright, pioneer and founder of the "real utopias project," in focusing on the institutions, organizations, and social movements that appear within capitalism but, at the same time, challenge its principles. I had worked with Erik in the early development of the project during the 1990s after the Soviet Union had dissolved and with it the very idea of an alternative to capitalism; it was a time when Francis Fukuyama was declaring the end of history, so new visions of what could be were urgently required. Now I am bringing his project into line with public sociology. After all, Erik elaborated the meaning of his real utopias through conversations with their practitioners, turning them into generalizable alternatives that could be widely disseminated. The task, however, is not only to elaborate these experiments as alternatives, but to connect them to each other as responses to marketization. While Erik's real utopias expand freedom, equality, and security, reactions to third-wave marketization can also move in the opposite direction. My colleague Arlie Hochschild, in her 2016 book, *Strangers in Their Own Land*, engages Tea Party supporters in Louisiana, trying to understand their very different responses to market-induced environmental degradation. Here the public sociologist wrestles with a reactionary utopia, with people who do not share her values. After four years of Trumpism and similar phenomena in so many other countries, engaging with right-wing movements has become imperative.

Third-wave marketization polarizes classes and politics, creating new audiences, clients, and partners for public sociology, but it is also transforming the very conditions of the production of knowledge and its reception in the public sphere. As I describe in the second chapter that follows, third-wave marketization is transforming the university, subjecting knowledge to commodification, turning it from a public good into a private enterprise in search of revenue. In attending to its fiscal crisis, the university generates governance, identity, and legitimation crises that can only be reversed through active reaffirmation of its public character. Sociology is well suited for this challenging task, not just in its engaged research but, as I shall argue in the last chapter, in its participatory pedagogy. The commodification of knowledge has yet to destroy this recalcitrant discipline whose roots lie in civil society, and whose raison d'être is to oppose the over-extension of market and state.

14

Third-Wave Marketization

At the height of his influence, with his extraordinary intellectual powers undiminished, Erik Olin Wright passed out of this world on January 23, 2019. We had been close friends for more than forty years, ever since he warned me of that fateful letter of "recommendation" from Edward Shils, which, by a curious turn of events, had landed me my job in Berkeley. Erik went off to the University of Wisconsin–Madison but we were in constant touch, regularly reading and commenting on each other's work. When it looked like I wasn't going to get tenure at Berkeley, he was a major force behind my getting a job at Madison. The unexpected reversal of the tenure denial saw me return to Berkeley a year later. Then a few years later Erik was offered a job at Berkeley. He visited for a year, but he too decided to return home, to Madison. As he put it, he preferred to be an intellectual among professionals rather than a professional among intellectuals. We continued to visit each other and meet in distant lands.

We had a common project – the revitalization of a scientific Marxism. Our styles of work were complementary – he used survey research to develop his class analysis whereas I used ethnography to develop the notion of production politics. He primarily studied the relations *of* production and only secondarily relations *in* production whereas I was the reverse, focusing on the relations *in* production against the backdrop of the relations *of* production. He moved toward international comparative research by mounting surveys across the world while I made the same move toward a global ethnography, becoming a worker in Hungary and then Russia, as well as collaborating with graduate students immersed in different countries.

In the beginning we took for granted the idea and the possibility of socialism, dissecting how capitalism reproduced itself despite and through its contradictions. With the collapse of communism, the very idea of a socialist alternative to capitalism became harder to sustain – capitalism had vanquished its challenger and history had come to end. Or so we were told. Erik turned from class analysis to pay ever increasing attention to what he called "real utopias," exploring socialist alternatives that emerged either through the self-transformation of capitalism or within the interstices of advanced capitalism, while I undertook a futile search for socialism in the wreckage of communism. For a time, we intended to write a book that would embrace our divergent experiences and perspectives but I was diverted by the project of public sociology and he went on to author his magnum opus, *Envisioning Real Utopias* (2010). Just before he died he finished a more popular version, *How To Be an Anticapitalist in the 21st Century* (2019). He had become a public sociologist par excellence.[4]

What are these "real utopias"? Where do they come from? Erik scoured the earth for institutions and organizations that posed a challenge to capitalism. They included participatory budgeting, which he first found in Porto Alegre, Brazil; universal basic income, which he found in Europe; cooperatives, which he found in all corners of the world; the collective self-organization of Wikipedia; the solidarity or social economy that he found in Quebec, bringing together daycare, elder care, disability care with recycling, performing arts, affordable housing, cooperatives – in short, a vibrant civil society. When the project began in the early 1990s, Erik worked from his office, reading about and then organizing symposia in Madison on a succession of "real utopias." As he started publishing and the project grew, he was invited to give talks in different countries and the project came to look more and more like "public sociology." He would spend time with the practitioners of real utopias, learning their history, the ins and outs of their projects, the dilemmas they faced, the conditions of their possibility and dissemination. From this raw data he would create an analytical model that could be lifted off the immediate context, a model that would then be discussed by practitioners and academics in conferences he organized. He was building a community of real utopians that transcended the university, engaged in very different projects but united in pursuit of a socialist future.

This was an organic public sociology – on-the-ground dialogue with the practitioners, elaborated into analytical models that were brought back to the practitioners, who were thereby connected to other real utopias. Over time Erik's audience became more skewed toward the practitioners themselves, who were excited by the broader meaning he brought to their uphill struggles on the ground. Erik had become an ethnographer, searching for prefigurative forms of socialism, analyzing them, handing them back to the community they came from, and then making them available to all.

Erik brought unity to his real utopias by tying them to a critique of capitalism and its transformation. He worked with a medical model: *diagnose the defects* of capitalism, *develop a treatment of real utopias*, and apply the treatment through *strategies of social transformation*. *Envisioning Real Utopias* ascribes the following defects to capitalism: it perpetuates eliminable human suffering, blocks human flourishing, limits individual freedom and autonomy, violates egalitarian principles of social justice, is inefficient and environmentally destructive, has systematic bias toward consumerism, promotes commodification that threatens broadly held values, fuels militarism and imperialism, corrodes community, and limits democracy.

To oppose these defects real utopias empower society vis-à-vis the state and market, building an imagination of socialism. But how can such real utopias be realized on a significant scale? Here Erik moves toward a general theory of social transformation that comes about through a combination of three strategies: through ruptural break with capitalism, through interstitial alternatives arising alongside capitalism, and through symbiotic compromises that were the unintended consequences of the reproduction of capitalism. In *How To Be an Anticapitalist in the 21st Century* Erik reformulates the strategies as dismantling, taming, resisting, and escaping capitalism, which combine to "erode" capitalism. Erik left us with the unfinished task of integrating these three dimensions – diagnosis, treatment, and strategy – as he still needed to show how real utopias emerge organically from the dynamics of capitalism, and to establish the conditions under which they lead to the social transformation of capitalism. To tackle this conundrum, Marxism requires some radical surgery. I will suggest we need to place the project of real utopias in the context of a Polanyian reconstruction of Marxism.

In the original Marxian model competition among capitalists leads to new techniques of extracting surplus labor from direct producers – that is, the intensification of exploitation. These new techniques – deskilling the labor process; introducing new technologies that entail further deskilling but also the displacement of labor; family labor that spreads the wage among two or more members of the household; migrant labor as a form of cheap labor – all lead to the polarization of rich and poor. This, in turn, gives rise to the deepening of class struggle on the one side and crises of overproduction and the concentration of capital on the other, eventually leading to the overthrow of capitalism. This model overlooks the key role of the state in reorganizing capitalism, so as to bring crises under control and contain class struggle. Ironically, where Marx and Engels thought that the working class was the gravedigger of capitalism, it turns out that the working class is the savior of capitalism – its struggles led to class compromise, to concessions that not only counteracted crises of overproduction but also cemented reformist politics and dampened the enthusiasm for revolution.

Today we may say that having a stable job is the privilege of a diminishing fraction of the working class, especially when considered globally. Precarity is a rising tide coming in from the Global South and engulfing more and more workers in the Global North. Remnants of a stable working class become a labor aristocracy, defending its declining privileges. It springs into action here and there, renewing hope for the extension of working-class struggle, but the overall trajectory is downward – whether we measure the trend by strikes, by union density, or by the strength of working-class parties. We require a theory of capitalism that does not rely on transcendent working-class struggles but unites them with other anticapitalist forces. For this we must move from *The Communist Manifesto* to Karl Polanyi's *The Great Transformation*.

In the previous chapter I drew on *The Great Transformation* to address Russia's catastrophic transition to capitalism. Russia may appear anomalous, but it exhibits, in extreme form, the pathologies of today's capitalism, giving Polanyi's theory general relevance. Polanyi's key move against Marxism was to focus the destructiveness of capitalism on the market rather than on production, on commodification rather than on exploitation, on exchange rather than on labor. Examining nineteenth-century England, he argues that the important working-class struggles – the factory movement for reduced working hours, the cooperative movement, and Robert Owen's communalism – were driven by opposition to the sale of labor power rather than to the exploitation of labor, struggles over the reproduction of labor power rather than the expenditure of labor. This provides Polanyi with an opening to extend the critique of capitalism to the way it turns three essential factors of production – labor, money, and land (nature) – into commodities subject to unregulated exchange.

These are "fictitious commodities" that were never intended to be commodities – so much so that turning them into commodities subject to unregulated exchange leads to the destruction of their use value. Indeed, in the extreme, these commodities are *ex-commodified*[5] – expelled from the realm of exchange, as when workers can no longer find a job, when the environment is destroyed, when money becomes increasingly a source of profit rather than a means of exchange and measure of value. We can add a fourth fictitious commodity, knowledge, whose commodification turns it from a public good advancing a public interest, into an instrument to expand commodification. In her book *The Age of Surveillance Capitalism* (2019) Shoshana Zuboff shows how our participation in the digital world, in social media, produces "data" that is processed into knowledge sold to capitalist moguls who thereby profit from the regulation of our lives. Further, the commodification of knowledge becomes an instrument to more effectively commodify labor, as in the gig economy; commodify money, as in the speculative debt economy; and commodify the environment, as in carbon trading. The commodification of knowledge intensifies the commodification and even ex-commodification of the other three fictitious commodities.

Polanyi's theory has an obvious resonance with the contemporary era but it had a fundamental flaw. Writing during World War II, Polanyi thought that humanity, having learned the lesson of the destructiveness of markets, would never again experiment with market fundamentalism. But he was wrong – beginning in the 1970s the world has been overwhelmed by another wave of marketization. Polanyi's error was to attribute market fundamentalism to human volition, to the dangerous utopianism of economists such as Hayek and von Mises. While they provide the ideology, the justification for market fundamentalism, it is capitalism that requires and regenerates markets to contain crises of profitability and overproduction. Extricating land, labor, money, and knowledge from their social integument and thereby subjecting them to commodification creates new markets and more profit.

This extrication or expropriation not only initiates capitalism as in Marx's "primitive accumulation," it is a continuing feature of capitalism, often violent, often generating social protest. David Harvey (2003) rightly makes much of this continuing "primitive accumulation" in his notion of "accumulation by dispossession." But are we witnessing "accumulation" or "disaccumulation"? Are the expropriations actually destroying capitalism rather than expanding it on the backs of the millions of displaced peasants, refugees, unemployed workers, evicted tenants and homeowners, victims of floods, fires, and pollution? Can we not say that markets are now in a mode of destroying capitalism, disaccumulation through dispossession, a process I earlier referred to as "involution"?

The reconstruction of *The Great Transformation* has to begin, therefore, with Polanyi's inability to anticipate another round of market fundamentalism tied to the destruction of capitalism. For Polanyi there is one long wave of marketization culminating in the crises of the 1930s that led to a *counter-movement* of state regulation – Stalinism, fascism, social democracy. Instead of one wave, I propose three waves of marketization, each with their distinctive counter-movements. The first wave defines early capitalism and generates counter-movements of a local character; the second wave calls forth a counter-movement centered on the state – organized capitalism or state socialism; while the third wave of marketization, what others call neoliberalism, has generated local and national reactions that have yet to summon up the global response necessary to fight international finance, climate change, and human displacement.

This Polanyi-inspired theory of capitalism offers a way of bringing real utopias under the umbrella of decommodification. Universal basic income (UBI) provides a meaningful basic subsistence existence for every adult that removes their dependence on a wage. It *decommodifies labor power*, enhancing the power of labor vis-à-vis capital, and provides the economic basis for other real utopias. Worker cooperatives in which workers both manage and own their enterprises would be more feasible if the state guarantees everyone a living wage. Even without UBI, cooperatives can offer security of employment unavailable to workers in capitalist enterprises. Erik's favorite cooperative, the huge Mondragon complex of worker cooperatives in the Basque country of Spain, is able to shuffle workers between units so as to keep many of them employed while unemployment soars in the wider society. Related to the survival of cooperatives is the availability of loans; for that we require public banks, sponsored by local communities accountable to the public rather than private interest. What is at stake is the *decommodification of money*, the regulation of its sale as credit to support community projects. Participatory budgeting is another real utopia involving decommodification in which a proportion of the municipal budget is distributed among public projects – schools, parks, roads, and so on – as decided by neighborhood councils in an elaborate democratic process. We have seen how third-wave marketization has exploited the commodification of knowledge but here, too, Erik emphasized real utopias involving "peer-to-peer" collaboration in such enterprises as Wikipedia. Another of Erik's favorites was the public library, another form of the *decommodification of knowledge*, making it freely available to all. Indeed, for Erik, the public library illustrates one principle behind the public ownership and organization of goods and services.

Erik has little to say about the commodification of nature but as Polanyi and Marx knew only too well this is the other side of the commodification of labor power. The working class, as a class of wage laborers, is produced by separating them from the land, which is thereby liberated for commodification. Land ownership becomes the basis of rural consolidation and dispossession, but also urban consolidation manifested in skyrocketing rents, evictions, and homelessness. In the rural areas cooperative farming and in the urban areas rent control or better public housing are forms of decommodification. Along with the commodification of land, there is the commodification of water and electricity, the creation and then profiteering from scarcity of the basic ingredients of human life. Centuries of plundering nature have given rise to new forms of commodification of the atmosphere through carbon trading, the sale of rights to pollute, which has failed to arrest global warming. We now learn that plundering nature is also a source of pandemics, exploited by Big Pharma, who make a killing from vaccines – a commodification of knowledge – developed after the spread of COVID-19. The Green New Deal is so far an imaginary utopia but it demonstrates what will be necessary to save the planet: it involves the radical trans-formation of capitalism, or more likely reimagining the meaning of socialism, whose condition will be the decom-modification of money, labor, and knowledge.

Erik's project is one of organic public sociology: engaging with real utopias through collaborations with their archi-tects and practitioners to elaborate their principles, to understand their mechanisms of expansion, to ferret out their contradictions, to explore the conditions of dissemination. It relies on the theories and methodologies of professional sociology, while also invigorating those theories; it deepens a critical sociology based on explicit values. Real utopias may be united in their reaction to third-wave marketization, projects of decommodification, but, at the same time, they are each propelled by their own distinctive normative foundations: equality-fairness, democracy-freedom, and community-solidarity. These are values touted by capitalism – recognized but not realized.

Taken as individual projects, real utopias represent reforms that maintain the capitalist ecosystem as a going concern – absorbing dissent and adapting to crisis. The goal of Erik's public sociology is to meld them into a singular unifying project – a reaction to third-wave marketization and, at the same time, pointing beyond capitalism – that captures the imagination of the dispossessed, forging a social movement for the "erosion" of capitalism. However, as in the reaction to second-wave marketization, so in the reaction to third-wave marketization there are authoritarian as well as democratic tendencies. Erik's real utopias aim to consolidate a socialist vision of an alternative future but what of the more right-wing populist movements? How does a public sociologist engage a very different politics than her own?

Arlie Hochschild (2016) spent five years with members of the Tea Party in Louisiana, 2011–16. Her book, *Strangers in Their Own Land,* sets out from a puzzle: why is it that victims of environmental degradation – the product of third-wave marketization – are so hostile to the state, the only institution that could regulate pollution, especially of the oil industry? As Raka Ray (2017) has argued, Hochschild's subjects harbor a subliminal understanding of Louisiana as a colony within the US, held to ransom by the profiteering practices of oil corporations. Yet rather than turn against the companies, rather than demand the state provide for their physical and economic security, they direct their animus to those who are "jumping ahead of them in the queue," minorities who are supposedly "privileged" by the state, immigrants flooding into the country to take their jobs. Having been neglected by the state, Tea Party supporters turn against those who are more marginal and vulnerable than themselves, people whom they have considered their inferiors. Even when Hochschild discovers community leaders who see the world as she does, they too have difficulty making inroads into the deeply entrenched common sense of a population fearing they will join the despised others at the bottom of society.

She sensitively but persistently engages with a view of the world so very different from her own. She struggles to climb the "empathy wall" that separates her from her subjects. She asks herself how it might be possible to redirect resentment targeting those they see as threatening toward the common enemy above. What are the crossover issues that might bring about a shared critique of their shared oppression? Under what conditions might the Green New Deal resonate with their lived experience? Can a project of decommodification have any meaning to Tea Party followers? These are the questions of the day tackled by such notable figures as Ruth Milkman (2020) and Chantal Mouffe (2018).

Can we redefine "decommodification" to attract broad popular support? What does decommodification mean today? In the first wave of marketization, decommodification focused on the self-destruction of the capitalist economy. Marxists paid little attention to the nature of socialism, the working class would make it themselves; it is not for intellectuals to design the specifics of socialism from above. In the second wave of marketization, decommodification was engineered by the state. This was the era of state socialism and social democracy in which the state substituted itself for the market. What then does decommodification mean under third-wave marketization, when the state is doing less to contain and more to promote the ravages of the market? The impetus for decommodification has to come from civil society. It doesn't mean that the state and market miraculously disappear; rather, they are subordinated to collective self-organization of civil society. It is a matter of restoring the social to socialism.

15

Whither the Public University?

For forty years I took the university for granted as a platform for research and teaching. In 2015 when my eight years with the International Sociological Association were over, I was invited to join the Board of the Berkeley Faculty Association (BFA). I had been a member for several years but paid little attention to its activities. Without the energy or desire to conduct fieldwork abroad, I thought joining the BFA Board would be an opportunity to return to my old interest in the university. Moreover, I knew I had benefited from the university in so many ways without paying my dues, without doing much service beyond the department. I was only six months on the board before Celeste Langan, my colleague from the English department, and I were dragooned into becoming the co-chairs of the organization. We were thrown in at the proverbial deep end to protest, as best we could, the ramifications of privatization.[6]

From the beginning I have relied on Chris Newfield's two books *Unmaking the Public University* (2008) and *The Great Mistake* (2016), which detail the folly of privatizing the public university, an account based on the University of California. His books are unequalled in their detail and in their vision of what has gone wrong. If I have any quibble with his analysis, it is the disposition toward voluntarism. Privatization was no more a "mistake" than climate change; privatization is the subsumption of the university to third-wave marketization, now ineluctably extended to the commodification of knowledge. This raises, once again, the two questions: "knowledge for whom?" and "knowledge for what?" In addressing ourselves we must ask how teaching and research should be organized, and in addressing others, should we prioritize narrow private interests or the more general public interest? My answers to these questions guide the organization of this chapter.

Unmaking the Public University

The Berkeley Faculty Association began in 1972 as a defense against aggressive moves by California's then governor, Ronald Reagan, aimed in particular at the Berkeley campus where student protests had been most prominent. University faculty were punished with cuts in salaries and in the campus budget. In the 1970s the BFA became a popular organization among the faculty to preserve the independence of the university, but thereafter it languished until its revitalization after the Great Recession and the faculty furloughs of 2009. It was then taken over by a more radical wing of the faculty, hostile to strategies of privatization driving the administration of the campus.

At the ten campuses that make up the University of California, faculty interests are formally represented by each campus's Academic Senate, whose long list of committees as well as its leadership are populated by an elected "committee on committees." In theory the Academic Senate partners with the campus administration – the Chancellor, the Vice-Chancellors, the Associate Vice-Chancellors, Provost and Vice-Provosts, the Deans, and so on – in "shared governance." Traditionally most administrators arose from the ranks of the faculty, and the Academic Senate became a common route into the administration. Over time the balance of power has shifted toward the administration, with the Senate acting as a rubber stamp. The BFA, on the other hand, is independent of both the Senate and the administration. It defends faculty interests but it is not a union: it does not bargain with management. We think of ourselves as the conscience of the Senate and, when we deem it necessary, as opposition to the campus administration.

A key point of contestation between the BFA and the campus administration continues to be the "privatization" of higher education. While the Berkeley campus was the original site of the University of California, which began in 1868 as a Land Grant College, it is now one of ten campuses. In the postwar expansion of higher education, the state of California promoted a particularly ambitious Master Plan that would provide free college education for all who desired it, in a three-tier system – two-year Community Colleges, the four-year California State University, and then an upper tier, the University of California with its flagship campuses at Berkeley and Los Angeles. If the 1960s were the height of public education, they were also, ironically enough, a period of burgeoning campus social movements. They began with Berkeley's 1964 Free Speech Movement attacking the mass university or what Clark Kerr, then President of the University, dubbed the multi-university (Kerr 1963). Today the three tiers still exist but the Master Plan with its vision of free education is in tatters. Clark Kerr, once the villain, target of student protest, has become a hero, a New Deal liberal who fought for public education.

Governor Reagan exploited the insurgent student movements – anti-war and civil rights – to arouse and mobilize popular sentiment against the University of California. He set the scene for the decline in public funding that can be traced to two events in 1978. The first was Proposition 13, which cut property taxes and thus state revenues. In the face of competing demands for expanded correctional facilities and rising costs of health, education – and especially higher education – was deemed politically expendable. The second significant event of 1978 was the Supreme Court ruling in the Bakke case against race-based quotas. The ruling did, however, still allow the university to use race as a factor in admissions. This set in motion affirmative action, and later the backlash against affirmative action, marked by the 1996 passage of California's Proposition 209. The two events of 1978 are connected: the diversification of admissions, in the eyes of what was still a largely white electorate, justified the withdrawal of public funding from the university.

One can debate the specific origins of the transformation of the University of California, but it is part of a national and indeed global trend, symptomatic of third-wave marketization, which turns what was once a public good into a private commodity. If knowledge used to be regarded as something produced and distributed for the benefit of all, it is now increasingly bought and sold by those who can afford it, so that the university becomes a revenue-generating machine, transforming its internal structure and threatening its national and international standing. For so long we thought of the public university as exempt from the forces of commodification. Yes, there were periodic crises that involved defunding, but they were always followed by restoration, albeit at a lower level. Too few were ready to acknowledge how the secular decline in funding was leading to the structural transformation of the university.

We can gauge the slow transformation of the university as a transition from "university in capitalist society" to the "capitalist university" – a move that is not specific to Berkeley or to the University of California. The "university in capitalist society" is a relatively autonomous institution, run by faculty for faculty, following the principles of shared governance and academic freedom. It is a monastic form of governance by privileged professionals, largely white and male, with security of employment (tenure), driven, in its own self-understanding, by the pursuit of truth. Its autonomy allows it to claim to represent the general interest of society by contributing subsidized research that lubricates capitalist accumulation, producing a professional managerial class and an educated citizenry. The research university generates a critical perspective toward elites that fail to live up to their espoused values. The "relatively autonomous" university doesn't exist in pure form; its independence was always subject to external pressures from corporate funders of research and agencies of the state. However, those pressures did not fundamentally alter its character. In the US the "relatively autonomous" university reached its peak in the boom of higher education during the two decades after World War II (Jencks and Riesman 1968). In those years the public university was seen to be a fundamental institution of modern society, leading such commentators as Daniel Bell (1973) to predict its centrality to the post-industrial society.

In the 1960s the US university spawned student protest – attacking the institution itself for its complicity in reproducing social, political, and economic ills at home and abroad. The public university contributed to the war in Vietnam, it excluded from its own ranks women and people of color, it limited freedom of speech in the name of university autonomy. The university became the focus of political backlash, temporarily casting off its cloak of complacency and questioning its projection as an ivory tower. It began to lose public funding, which led to the pursuit of new sources of revenue, the commodification of knowledge that, in turn, led to its slow transformation. It came to look ever more like a capitalist corporation with an enlarged managerial structure imposing itself on faculty and students alike. The transition to a "capitalist university" is still ongoing, thereby generating a succession of mutually reinforcing crises: fiscal, governance, identity, and legitimation. Using Berkeley as my case study I will sketch out these crises as a function of third-wave marketization.

Fiscal Crisis

In the conventional account, defunding public education set in motion compensating increases in student tuition. Newfield (2016) offers an alternative explanation – suggesting that the public university contributed to its own demise by raising student tuition to cover increasing costs of research. In this view it was the university that triggered the spiraling tuition increases with the withdrawal of state support. Whatever the cause, the University of California increased undergraduate tuition from a nominal sum of $150 per year in 1970 to today's $15,000 for California residents and more than twice as much for out-of-state or international students. In the academic year 2010–11, for the first time, revenue from student tuition and fees exceeded funding from the state of California. By 2018–19 tuition and fees amounted to 32 percent of campus revenue while the state's contribution to campus revenue amounted to only 15 percent.

Still, any increase in student tuition had to be approved by the state legislature – tuition was limited to $15,000 between 2015 and 2020. Those whose parental income was less than $80,000 did not pay any tuition and it was reduced for those whose parents together earned less than $120,000 per annum. The campus circumvented these constraints by parlaying its reputation into enrollment of out-of-state and international students who paid twice the in-state tuition and fees. In the twenty years from 1999 to 2019 enrollment of California students fell from 82 percent to 67 percent. Alarmed that outsiders were taking up precious spaces in California's public university, the state insisted on limits on the overall percentage of out-of-state students, which was accomplished through unprecedented increases in enrollments at already overcrowded campuses.

After reaching the limits of one source of revenue another is pursued. Thus, another strategy has been to develop special programs – self-financing MA programs or professional certificates in business or engineering. Other departments devise one-off fee-paying courses in the summer, often online, to bring in badly needed funds. My own department hit upon the idea of enticing students from abroad for a semester, charging them substantial fees for "concurrent enrollment." These innovations in the commodification of knowledge bring in funds in the short term until everyone catches on, competition increases, and revenue falls. Or a pandemic strikes and "concurrent enrollment" disappears overnight.

As these alternative sources of revenue are choked off, the university turns to its alumni and other "friends" in capital campaigns. Accustomed to state funding, Berkeley like other public universities was a latecomer to building an endowment. Even when successful it had its limits, if only because of the restricted use of funds. For example, donors like to give money for a new building to be named after them, but the funds are often inadequate and the university is left carrying additional costs as well as maintenance. Corporate investment in cheap research can also be costly for the university. For example, after much controversy, Berkeley accepted a $350 million investment from British Petroleum to create an Energy Biosciences Institute. The university put up money for a new building, but was left holding the bag when BP unceremoniously pulled out after the Deepwater Horizon oil spill in the Gulf. The university is so desperate for funds that it strikes deals, so called public–private partnerships, which create credit in the short run but can be very costly in the long run. Privatization digs the university into deeper debt (Newfield 2016).

The commodification of prestige and knowledge is one strategy; the commodification of labor is another. Universities can go after the weak and the vulnerable, outsourcing low paid service work to avoid paying benefits or even minimum wages. Economic restructuring led to dramatic change in teaching as expensive tenure-track faculty have been replaced by short-term, precarious instructional labor, known variously as lecturers, adjuncts, and part-time or contingent faculty. When I began teaching at Berkeley, lecturers barely existed; today they teach some 40 percent of student credit hours. Across higher education lecturers now outnumber tenure-track faculty by two to one, whereas fifty years ago the ratio was the inverse. As the number of tenure-track positions declines, the oversupply of PhDs has left them competing for low-paid, insecure teaching positions. The conditions of lecturers vary a great deal across higher education, depending on the status of their employer, but every-where their conditions of employment are vastly inferior to tenure-track faculty who, thereby, are released from teaching to conduct research. In the short run, tenured and nontenured faculty have opposed interests; in the long run they have a common interest in stemming the degradation of the public university.

Governance Crisis

As commodification makes inroads into the university, it brings about changes in the administrative structure. Fiscal crisis has been accompanied by "administrative bloat." According to the university's figures, the number of senior and executive managers at Berkeley increased five-fold in the twenty years from 1994 to 2014, so that they now equal the number of tenure-track faculty, which has remained constant over the same period. It's not just the numbers but also the salaries. A senate committee reported that between 2010 and 2015 salaries of Berkeley's central administration increased by 38 percent whereas the income of academic units increased by 13 percent. While Berkeley is at the extreme, we can find similar adminis-trative expansion at the other University of California campuses and indeed across higher education.

Coincident with administrative expansion has been the recruitment of executives from the financial and corporate world. For example, Berkeley's Vice-Chancellor for Finance and Administration came from the World Bank, knowing little about the operation of universities, let alone the peculiarities of a public university like Berkeley. He recruited personnel from the world of finance to help him govern the university. He lasted for five years. The university attracts such "spiralists" who enter the university from outside, perhaps from the corporate world, develop their own signature project and then spiral on (if they are lucky), leaving the university, saddled with debt, to spiral down. In this case the Vice-Chancellor tried to promote "online" education, which proved to be an expensive flop, and he spiraled out and down.

After the economic crisis of 2008–9 that left the campus in dire straits, the Chancellor at the time called on outside consultants Bain and Company to identify ways the university could save money. Bain charged the campus $7.5 million for developing a plan for restructuring the campus that would cost a further $70 million to implement. The report, called *Operational Excellence*, identified a number of inefficiencies: too many layers of management, supervisors with too limited a span of control, and too much duplication in managerial operations. The plan called for a new system of management, Campus Shared Services, that would reduce the "duplication" of administrative staff by pulling them out of departments and relocating them in distant offices. This proved to be neither operational nor excellent, breaking the close connection between faculty and department staff, who held the tacit knowledge necessary for managing research projects, teaching curriculum, and employment of students. As staff were relocated, departments had to hire extra personnel to administer projects that required close and continuous collaboration within departments. Campus Shared Services was declared a failure after three years.

This was just one ill-conceived project designed to cut costs that had the opposite effect. Perhaps the most famous sinkhole was the seismic retrofit of Berkeley's football stadium. Campus engineers considered it impossible to retrofit the stadium to withstand a major earthquake, but the project moved ahead. When it was planned, again just after the Great Recession, it was to be financed by alumni paying from $40,000 to $225,000 for special reserved seats that they would hold for fifty years. The venture was a financial disaster; alumni were not interested in paying exorbitant amounts to watch a losing football team. In the end the retrofit would cost $445 million and the campus would be saddled with an annual $18 million debt, rising to an estimated $37 million a year by 2044.

Having overseen failed attempts at reversing fiscal crisis and mishandling the student protests in 2009 following the 32 percent increase in tuition, the Chancellor resigned in 2013. He was succeeded by another outsider. He too had his signature project – to build a Global Campus not far from Berkeley, on vacant land deemed environmentally hazardous. Instead of building campuses in the Middle East or Asia, Berkeley would use its "brand" to attract investment from major foreign universities to build a local international campus. Before the project had a chance to demonstrate its folly, after three years in office, the Chancellor resigned under pressure of faculty, appalled by the cover-up of cases of sexual harassment, openly justified in the name of upholding Berkeley's "reputation"! As a spiralist this Chancellor built a fence around himself – figuratively and literally – keeping faculty and students at a distance. Instead of asking a local to be his deputy, he installed an Executive Vice-Chancellor from another university, a private one. Instead of using the wisdom of faculty and students, he hired outside consultants to guide his plans.

Sobered by a succession of disasters, the Board of Regents chose a "local" for the next Chancellor. She had been a faculty member at Berkeley since 1970 and became Executive Vice-Chancellor before moving on to become President of Smith College. After ten years she returned to Berkeley to retire, but was pulled back in as interim

Executive Vice-Chancellor as a stopgap measure to clean up the mess left by her predecessors. The campus breathed a sigh of relief when she was appointed Chancellor. Convinced that privatization was the only strategy going forward, she pursued it deliberately and rationally. Her first goal was to eliminate the burgeoning annual deficit of some $150 million by multiplying revenue streams as well as trimming expenses. With soaring rents it was increasingly difficult for students and faculty to live in Berkeley or the surrounding areas, so she set about expanding university accommodations through public-private partnerships.

The smoother operation of the new regime throws into relief what is taken for granted – the progressive commodification of knowledge, keeping the university alive with privatization strategies, even to the point of openly repudiating support for tuition-free education. With a disastrous credit rating, due to the fiascos of the past, the administration is forced into high-risk investments, often over opposition from faculty. The restructuring of the administration has gradually expropriated control from all campus communities – faculty, lecturers, staff, students. Leaving the hallowed value of shared governance, we have entered a regime of consultative governance – consultations after the fact – driven by market forces.

Identity Crisis

Increasingly focused on making money to stem its fiscal crisis, the university administration undermines collective self-government, bringing on a governance crisis, which in turn prompts an identity crisis. Are we a private or a public institution, responsive to particular interests or generational interests, reproducing or challenging the commodification of knowledge?

The university divides into competing sectors. Some regions of the university are better able to exploit the marketplace than others. The biosciences and engineering supply research allied to expanding regions of the economy; the business and law schools supply managers and regulators; schools of public policy and social welfare supply the expertise to administer and treat precarious populations. As tuition increased and employment prospects dimmed, so students gravitate toward those disciplines that supply the best job opportunities, whether that be a path to a professional degree or directly into the more secure regions of the labor force. The university surreptitiously pushes toward vocationalism at the expense of a broad liberal education. The number of majors in the arts and humanities falls. The university follows student demand by redistributing resources among departments on the basis of "student credit hours" and the number of degrees. In a time of shrinking budgets the competition between departments becomes palpable, no longer on the basis of scholarly distinction but on their appeal to students.

The capitalist university not only creates lateral inequalities between disciplines but also vertical ones. As we have seen, cutting costs means employing armies of lecturers to do the teaching abdicated by a relatively shrinking labor aristocracy of tenure-track faculty. At a prestigious public university, tenure-track faculty create the symbolic capital of the university – the number of prominent scholars, Nobel Prize winners, as well as turning out outstanding graduate students. The tenure-track faculty are pampered with diminished teaching loads and off-scale salaries in order to keep up with Ivy League universities. The capitalist university creates an entrenched two-tier system – a lower caste of dedicated teachers and an upper caste of researchers. There is virtually no mobility between the two. In the short term, the interests of the tenure-track faculty lie in the multiplication of lecturers, but in the long term they suffer declining numbers. Graduate students, expecting to enter the ranks of tenure-track faculty, now face two tracks into the future (Burawoy and Johnson-Hanks 2018).

The Berkeley Faculty Association defends the idea of the public university, opposing privatization, the corporatization of the university, the commodification of knowledge. In practice this means we oppose economically irrational projects (public–private ventures, retrofitting the stadium, privileging athletics, campus shared services), the degradation of education through online education, and revenue-making credentials with limited content. It means we support diversity at all levels of the campus, defend shared governance, build alliances with unions of graduate student instructors (GSIs), lecturers, and staff. The BFA along with other University of California faculty associations has thrown its weight behind a plan to refinance higher education from increases in state taxation. Rather than pursuing the self-destructive strategies of privatization, we support the "$66 fix" – $66 being the extra tax a median income earner in California would pay in order to reset higher education to funding levels of the year 2000. This has the support of a wide range of unions and associations involved with higher education, though it has yet to win the broad support of California's population or the political establishment that runs the state.

Legitimation Crisis

Accustomed to support from the state legislature as one of California's symbols of progress, the university has experienced a slow downgrading for some fifty years. It is now one of many public agencies competing for a diminishing slice of the state budget. State funding per student has fallen steadily over the last fifty years at the same time that fees have increased. Here lies one material reason for the declining public support for the university. As student fees increase, as total costs of attendance increase at an even greater rate, and as the degree itself buys less lucrative, more precarious jobs, so many wonder whether university education is worth the increasing cost.

It may be necessary but not sufficient for an economically secure future. As college education has become part of an individual or family strategy to advance a person's career, so the university as a collective public good recedes into the background. The more families pay for their children's education, the less they want their taxes going to the same university.

To the public the university's claim to be in perpetual economic crisis seems bogus in the light of rising tuition but also in the light of the media attention given to scandals that have swirled around the university: sexual harassment by the high and mighty, bribing one's way into the university, misuse of funds by the Office of the President, increasing numbers of out-of-state and international students displacing Californians of equal or greater scholarly merit, exorbitant salaries of administrators, abysmal conditions of service employees receiving subminimum wages. Uninterested in its "international" prestige, Governor Jerry Brown wanted the university to mimic his favorite fast-food chain Chipotle Mexican Grill: the university should offer a low-cost fixed menu of courses. The public looks at the university through a different lens than its administrators and its faculty.

In one area, at least, the University of California has had some success in deepening its public character: namely, the broader access to the university, whether by class or by race. *The New York Times* annual listing of universities that are most effective at promoting social mobility regularly puts the University of California and its campuses at or near the top. At Berkeley from 2000 to 2020 first-generation students increased from 7 percent to 26 percent, and "under-represented minorities" (the university's category) increased from 13 percent to 20 percent (but African American students are still only 3.7 percent of the total). Berkeley has far fewer "under-represented minorities" than other campuses: Berkeley's figure of 20 percent compares to Riverside's 42 percent and at Merced, the newest campus, the figure is 60 percent. As Hamilton and Nielsen (2021) show, Riverside and Merced are also the less well-resourced campuses. More generally, as the number of students of color and students from poorer backgrounds have increased, the resources available for education have diminished and costs of attendance have increased – students are getting less but paying more (Samuels 2013).

In short, it is not enough to think only of access. We also need to think of what happens to students once they arrive on campus. The university needs to be accessible but also accountable, and not just to its students but also to communities outside the university. Reversing the legitimation crisis requires us to extend ourselves into the wider communities from which students come. It requires us to reconceive the place of the university in the wider society. Berkeley has made efforts in this direction, building programs of scholarly engagement, but they are poorly funded and marginal to the university's overall program. The university cannot survive as an ivory tower.

The Future

When COVID-19 struck, Berkeley, like other universities, was plunged into darkness and mounting deficits. The university was quick to understand on which side its bread was buttered. It could do without Nobel Prize winners, but not without students. As in-person teaching became impossible, administrators worried if students would be prepared to enroll for remote instruction, charging the same fees. Suddenly, teaching took priority and during the summer of 2020, there were endless websites, workshops, seminars on the "best practices" for remote instruction. The tables were turned: the inessential and taken for granted became the essential raison d'être of the university. As it happened, students came roaring back in the fall, only too happy to regain some order in their disjointed lives, even though it meant the disappearance of campus life. An empty campus is still very costly. Berkeley posted an anticipated loss of $340 million (about 15 percent of the annual budget) by the end of the 2020–2021 academic year – losses from dining, housing, entertainment, athletics, and other auxiliary ventures, as well as the extra costs of remote instruction. The question now haunts instruction as to what pressures will be brought to bear – and on whom – to continue online education, now that faculty and students have had to learn how to live with it.

As in so many sectors of society, COVID-19 is likely to be the catalyst of further polarization of an already steeply hierarchical system of higher education. Many colleges will not be able to recover from the accumulating losses and will disappear or descend toward a degraded vocational education so effectively described by Tressie McMillan Cottom in her book *Lower Ed* (2017). Already well-practiced in online education, for-profit colleges will have competitive advantages over traditional in-person education, which will be reserved for elite colleges and universities. Certainly the Ivy League universities will survive, but which of the public universities will also survive, and under what conditions, is less clear.

Polarization will not only affect the system as a whole, but for those that survive it is likely to divide the university itself, deepening trends already in motion. A burgeoning administrative structure will rule over the increased separation of teaching from research. As at Berkeley, so elsewhere, overworked and underpaid lecturers are slowly taking over teaching undergraduates while a labor aristocracy of tenure-track faculty spend more of their time doing research, working with diminishing numbers of graduate students, and supporting new "revenue streams." Under this dispensation, one wonders how many students will devote six to ten years to obtain a PhD for the insecurity of contingent employment? So the lecturers themselves will diminish in quality. As research and teaching diverge, they may no longer take place under the same roof, as research migrates out of the university into independent institutes and think tanks. The university will no longer offer subsidized research for the general good; instead, research will increasingly serve those who can pay for it.

Unless there is a counter-movement against the global reach of third-wave marketization, the same pressures for commodification will infect universities in all corners of the world. Indeed, the process is already far gone in many places, especially in poorer countries. Thus, my alma mater, the University of Zambia, is heavily in debt, bulging with some 20,000 fee-paying students taught by precariously employed instructors experiencing regular pay arrears – a far cry from the proud institution I knew in 1970–72. The larger and richer nations of the Global South, such as Brazil, South Africa, and India, are able to concentrate resources into one or two flagship national universities, while the rest become credentialing mills. The university has lost its symbolic status as a mark of progress and nationhood, allowed to decay in so many places, and restructured as a capitalist enterprise in others.

These are the dystopian tendencies that have overtaken the American university, but we should not forget the 1960s assault on the university came out of the blue. It was a protest movement inspired by the blatant injustices of the world beyond, injustices mirrored in the operation of the university. As I write we are still in the midst of the pandemic that has clarified the injustices of today, also mirrored in the university. It has become clear who is carrying the burden of the university, namely the very ones who are supposed to benefit from the university. Just as in 1964, so now it is difficult to imagine fundamental challenges to the ascendancy of the capitalist university. Still the university remains the one institution that, in principle, might be able to conceive of an alternative world, the one institution that can see and tackle the destructive forces that have overtaken the planet, the one institution that can nurture and make itself accountable to a universal, public interest.

16

Living Theory

It's January 1977. I have won the lottery and landed a job at Berkeley – the job of dreams. Neil Smelser had overseen my appointment and, as chair, decided that I should teach the required undergraduate course in social theory. There was not a lot of enthusiasm for teaching theory, indeed there was not a lot of enthusiasm for teaching in those days, so being a new recruit I was given the assignment. In graduate school my grades for theory were in the B and C range, so it was ironic that I had been chosen for the task. It was not clear who was being punished – the students or myself. But, for me at least, it proved to be a stroke of good fortune. I've been teaching social theory ever since.

With much trepidation and blessed with two wonderful teaching assistants, Anne Lawrence and Bob Fitzgerald, I diligently prepared to teach the "classics." That January, I walked into the lecture hall that could hold many more than the sixty students scattered among the seats. I told them I was new to teaching; I had never even been an undergraduate in the US. I announced that we were going to learn social theory together through the lens of the "division of labor" – a topic consonant with my own interests, a theme that threaded through the classics, and a phenomenon central to their own lives. I then had the presence of mind to ask them what they thought was meant by the "division of labor." As the seconds ticked away and they found the silence unbearable, someone offered an answer, and then someone else, and soon they were competing for my attention. Although I didn't know it at the time, this was the beginning of a long experiment in teaching as public sociology.

Students after all are our first public. We may be fond of research, we may even be good at research, we may make breakthroughs in research, and the university may reward research above all else, but, in most cases, our lasting impact lies with our students. That impact is all the deeper if we can speak to their lived experience, transforming how they regard themselves and how they see the world around them. These are after all their formative years. The appeal of sociology lies in the way it speaks directly to that lived experience, especially when the students themselves come from more marginalized sectors of society.

As the university drew in more students from under-privileged backgrounds, from racial minorities and first-generation students, it is not surprising that the sociology major expanded. "Under-represented minor-ities" are now 38 percent of our sociology major, twice the campus average; and more than half our students are transfers from two-year community colleges, as compared to the campus average of less than a third. Sociology has expanded from 150 to 600 majors, and the theory course is now taught twice a year, with some 200 students in each class – non-majors can't even get in. The course itself expanded from a required one quarter to two quarters to two semesters. And for social theory addicts there is even a voluntary third semester.

The department has changed over the last half-century; it has become more professionalized and less grandiose. My tenure-track colleagues are committed to teaching and we have a brilliant group of dedicated lecturers (non-tenure-track faculty). Teachers are more respectful of students, entering into a dialogue about their lives through the lens of immigration, race and ethnicity, gender, family, political economy, poverty, incarceration, work, policing, schooling, and much else. Courses develop under an overarching reality – the soaring inequality that has been overwhelming society for the last half-century. The students can see themselves – their past, their present, and the future – in the courses we teach.

If teaching substantive topics can easily become public sociology, what about social theory? How can one make the dead white men of the nineteenth century – Marx, Weber, and Durkheim – live in the eyes and imagination of twenty-first century undergraduates? How can the great thinkers of the past speak to the lived experience of today? Social theory is conventionally taught as a survey of canonical thinkers, sometimes based on original texts, sometimes on textbooks, but the idea is to give a flavor of "grand theorists" with big ideas. That's how I began. In one quarter I tried to cover the gamut of theorists from Adam Smith to Jürgen Habermas via Marx and Engels, Comte, Spencer, Durkheim, and Weber. It was an impossible task.

The *survey* approach offers a panorama, a mountain range, seen from a distance, but it doesn't give students the chance to climb any of those mountains and witness the vistas they offer. I simply did not have the wherewithal – the knowledge of history and philosophy – to undertake a serious survey course, and even if I did it would be difficult to convey such themes in a quarter-long course. I had to adopt a very different *ethnographic* approach that starts out by bringing student lives into social theory with the aim of bringing social theory into their lives. I call it *living theory* – theory itself lives, it is dynamic and transcendent, just as students live in theory, shaping their imagination of who they are and what the world could be.

We start by thinking of social theory as a cognitive map. Maps simplify the world but from a particular perspective through different projections; different maps have different purposes; you have to learn how to read maps; they have predictive power and guide action; some maps are more accurate, some more comprehensive than others; maps are redrawn in the light of the knowledge they generate. So the same may be said of social theories: they too are simplifications, have different purposes, guide human action, are more or less accurate, more or less comprehensive, and so on. Like maps, social theories affect the world they represent; they lead us to intervene in the world they represent – that is what we mean by public sociology.

I also liken social theory to a lens without which we cannot see the world we inhabit. As members of society, we share a common lens that we call "common sense." Without that shared lens, that shared theory – of which language is its most basic form – we could not live together. In other words, we are all carriers of social theory. To be a social theorist is to reflect on that common sense, elaborate it, transform it. Sociological theory is a special type of social theory. It sees the world as a problem, a world that is less than perfect, a world that could be different. Sociological theory questions what we take for granted. It challenges common sense, showing the partiality of its truth, how in our daily lives we misrecognize what we are up to. Under the spell of sociological theory, "common sense" is transformed from something natural and inevitable into something socially constructed (and durably so), and thus artificial and arbitrary. Understood in this way, sociological theory is always public sociology, challenging the common sense we take for granted.

That's all very well in principle but what about in practice? How can we bring those nineteenth-century lofty theorists to ground, make them accessible and meaningful to twenty-first-century undergraduates? My first strategy is to read all the theorists through some familiar idea or experience – the notion of the division of labor, say, a concept central to all sociological theory but also to everyone's life. The second strategy is to carefully select limited extracts from each theorist – a few pages for each lecture – with a view to slowly building up their theories from first principles. We start with a theory's basic assumptions about individuals, society, and history, gradually working our way toward a theory of the division of labor – its origins and its consequences, its reproduction and its future. At every step of the way we are illustrating each concept, each connection, each assumption with reference to the empirical world.

Sticking to texts, we slowly put together the pieces in a jigsaw until we have a picture – literally a pictorial representation of each theory. It might take weeks, but students partake in every move. Through their participation they can see before them the construction of a building from the foundation up. Every lecture is an emergent picture, drawn with chalk on a blackboard. At the end they see that the house of theory can be rather unstable, and we need to pull it apart and rebuild it or add extensions that fit in with the overall architecture. In calling attention to anomalies, false inferences about the world, and the contradictions they may reflect, we are "ransacking" theory; but no ransacking is done without rebuilding. Every great theory has great contradictions, but if the theory is really "great" then it can be redeemed through wrestling with those contradictions. That is the work of theory.

That's what happens in the lecture hall. But the entire enterprise would be very different were it not for the dedication of the five or six teaching assistants, now known as Graduate Student Instructors. They run two discussion sections that meet twice a week for fifty minutes. Each section used to have fifteen students but then it was increased to twenty. That's where students engage with theory. That's where they practice dissecting a sentence, a paragraph; that's where they practice putting theories together and putting them into conversation with one another; that's where they apply theories to the world around them. It is in section that students will have their most memorable experiences, providing a platform for their own spontaneous discussion groups. The participatory ethos is further cultivated by my weekly meetings with the GSIs where we discuss specific challenges, problem cases, and have exciting debates about ambiguous texts. Every Thursday evening we assemble in my office at 6 p.m., finish at 8 p.m., and then go to dinner. When it comes to theory, they quickly learn there is no better teacher than teaching.[7]

Participation in sections contributes some 20 percent or 25 percent of the student grade, and that's where students prepare themselves for their assignments. There are no exams or quizzes, but a series of short 750-word papers that require students to explicate theories by comparing them along specified dimensions, or by showing how different theories offer different interpretations of a short, descriptively rich article taken from the world of journalism – *The New York Times*, *The Wall Street Journal*, *The New Yorker*, and so on. Once a semester, students write their own short "theory in action paper" – choosing a phenomenon to be illustrated by one or more of the theories they have learned. Sometimes, under the inspiration of a GSI, they collaborate in generating a sequence of theory-in-action papers, engaging the drama of the world around them through the lenses of successive theories. In the fall of 2008, for example, GSIs got students to write brief memos showing the ways social theories illuminated the deep economic crisis and then the election of the first African American President. In these ways it becomes clear how these theories from a century or more ago transcend their times, have relevance today, thereby making their originators canonical figures.

So which theorists do we read? Since the theme is the division of labor, we start with the opening twenty pages of Adam Smith's *The Wealth of Nations*. Here we have an admirable point of departure – a simple and lucid theory of the division of labor in which specialization leads to greater productivity through time-saving, dexterity, and innovation – a potential that is realized with the extension of demand for excess supply – that is, with the expansion of the market. As a result, we get the "wealth of nations" or what Smith also calls "universal opulence" – that is, everyone is better off as a result of the division of labor, but under certain conditions, namely, "a well-governed society." In bolstering his utopian view, Smith appeals to our intuition by telling a story of its origins in a small-scale society of hunters and gatherers, how if hunters specialize and gatherers specialize they will each produce more and through "truck, barter and exchange" everyone will be better off.

Simple, appealing, but what are its flaws? Today, are people better off as a result of increased productivity? Students are suspicious, even more suspicious when I produce a graph of increasing productivity and declining real wages. So what's the problem? It's Smith's assumption that individuals control the surplus they produce. So what happens to the surplus if it is not owned and controlled by the person who produces it? Enter Marx, whose theory of the division of labor centers not only on the question of specialization, "Who Does What?" but also on who owns the surplus, "Who Gets What?" – out of which will emerge his theory of the rise and fall of capitalism, his theory of class struggle and the transition to communism.

But Smith makes other assumptions, too, in order to get his theory to work: "universal opulence" comes from individuals in pursuit of their material self-interest, all endowed with the same resources, embedded in relations of power equality. These "common sense" assumptions are examined in Durkheim's theory that connects the division of labor to *solidarity* and by Weber's theory that connects division of labor to *authority*. It's not difficult to show how Smith's theory of the division of labor, first published in 1776, the year of American Independence, is still widely believed today, in fact more than ever. It is the foundation of the American ideology – that by striving individuals can make it. By interrogating Smith one is entering the heart of the dominant belief system. A course in social theory is not confined to theories critical of society, but includes the power of theories to legitimate society. We learn much about the dominant ideology when we ask how Smith handles the gender division of labor, the future of slavery, or relations between nations.[8]

The ethnographic approach to social theory not only brings social theory into the lives of students, but it brings theories into a dialogue with one another. In the first semester, as a response to Smith, we develop the Marxist tradition, starting with six weeks of Marx and Engels, followed by two weeks each of Lenin, Gramsci, and Fanon. We construct Marx and Engels's theory from first principles enunciated in *The German Ideology*, proceeding to their theory of capitalism and its self-transformation advanced in *Wage Labour and Capital, Socialism: Scientific and Utopian*, and *The Communist Manifesto* – all to be found in Robert Tucker's (1978) *The Marx–Engels Reader*. Once we have created the architecture, we then ransack the theory, arriving at three fundamental flaws: an undeveloped theory of the state, a false theory of class struggle, and an absent theory of transition from capitalism to communism. From the critique of Marx and Engels we turn to reconstruction, engaging two flaws at a time. Facing the prospects of the Russian Revolution in 1917, Lenin writes *State and Revolution* interrogating the relation between state and transition; facing the absence of the predicted revolution in the West, Gramsci tackles the state and class struggle; and facing the prospects of the postcolonial future, Fanon tackles class struggle and transition. Each of these reconstructions calls forth further questions and anomalies.

Here we confront the "dialectics" of public sociology: how theoretically informed political practice contributes to changes in the world that feed back into sociological theory, requiring further theoretical revision. The life of theory reflects its engagement with the changing world it describes. At the end of the first semester I present students with a series of short articles on some transformative event in world history – anti-apartheid struggles or the Marikana massacre in South Africa, the Russian Revolution, Nicaraguan Revolution, Cuban Revolution, Zapatista movement in Mexico, the civil rights movement in the

US, the struggle of Palestinians against Israeli domination, and so on. They write four short essays showing how the theories of Marx and Engels, Lenin, Gramsci, and Fanon come alive in interpreting these historic moments.

If the first semester is the constitution of a theoretical tradition, the second semester is the clash of theoretical traditions, contestations that are not in any text but are created in the lecture hall, forcing students to evaluate competing theories against the world they know but also worlds they do not know, described in films and journalism. Again we read carefully selected excerpts from the chosen theorists for building their distinctive theory of the division of labor, so that we can then relate them back to the theories of the first semester. Thus, Durkheim faces off against Marx and Engels on the morality and future of the division of labor; Weber faces off against Lenin on the durability and future of bureaucracy; Foucault faces off against Gramsci on the relationship between state and civil society.

During the spring, the world often enters the lecture hall with campus protests. In my early years organizers for small revolutionary parties would invade the lecture hall, push me aside, and take over the class. I'd fight back and students and their GSIs would rise up to defend their benighted professor. Nothing like an invasion to build unity! More usually it's politics outside the classroom that attracts student attention – a strike by GSIs, a rally by Black Lives Matter, support for exploited lecturers. Here's a typical moment. It's 2011, the campus is in turmoil, the Occupy Movement is flexing its muscle. A student wanders into the class fifteen minutes late, interrupts me, and announces that a classmate has chained himself to the top of a building in protest against increases in student tuition. "Let's go and support him," she shouts. I turn to the class. We discuss what to do. Many are enthusiastic, others resentful, I strike a compromise – let's take the class to the picket lines and continue there. We are moving from Weber to Foucault so it's not difficult to bring theory to life on the picket line – reading from the texts, using the public microphone, hundreds of us ask whether the university is a bureaucracy or a prison. Others join the discussion, curious about what we are up to. Theory in action!

The last part of the course is the development of a feminist tradition – Simone de Beauvoir (1949), Catharine MacKinnon (1982), and Patricia Hill Collins (1986) – that not only points to gender blindness but also turns the course upside down and inside out, by questioning the so-called objectivity of the theorists whose place in society shapes the way they see the world. Feminist theory claims that social theory is not only about capturing the nature of the world out there; it is also about the location of the theorist who constructs an understanding of the world from a certain vantage point. Social theorists are not astronomers mapping the universe; it matters that they are in the world they are theorizing. Smith, Marx, Engels, Durkheim, and Weber are not impartial observers offering competing theories, they are partial participants in a world they construct from different standpoints. Feminist theory throws the world back into the face of the student, forcing them to interrogate their own life from the standpoint of their gender and sexuality, then their race or their class. Theory has come home: from students of theory they become producers of theory. The last assignment is to construct their own map – a poster that summarizes the entire year-long course, illuminating the connections among the theorists through the lens of feminist theory. In a final twenty-minute conversation with their teaching assistant students present and defend their pictorial representation. I have a museum of the art of theory.

To treat teaching as public sociology is to think of students as a public, carrying a vision of who they are and how the world works. They are not empty vessels into which we pour pearls of wisdom, but living, sentient beings who are always thinking about the world around them and how they fit into it. Even if they don't see it in sociological terms, they are always thinking about their place in the division of labor. I try to bring that thinking to the surface. A theory course based on the division of labor opens students' eyes to different meanings and dimensions, not only of the division of labor but also of their own lives.

Public sociology does not succeed by simply postulating alternative visions. It succeeds by bringing participants into four dialogues: the first is a dialogue between teacher and student that sets up the parameters of the course; the second is a dialogue between teaching assistant and students that brings theory to the world in which they live; the third is a dialogue among students in class and section but also around the succession of assignments and papers where they rediscover who they are; the fourth dialogue, the most ambitious one, carries social theory into the world beyond as they interact with fellow students, with family and with friends. This, at any rate, is the vision that I seek to realize.

I exploit my advantage – students are a captive public, consent backed up by force. They need the credential, the grade that means they are their own audience for two semesters, or, more broadly, for four years in which they are bombarded with interpretations of the world they inhabit. Public sociology in the world beyond is so much harder. Out there conveying sociology is intermittent at best – an interview, an opinion piece, an essay, a book – there is little that is systematic. Moreover, sociology faces competition from other disciplines, as well as from journalism, from film and television, and from social media. The public sphere is a terrain of power; because it competes with and disrupts common sense, sociology is near the bottom of the totem pole. In moments of crisis when common sense is shattered, then the space for sociology potentially widens.

And that's just the situation I face now in the fall of 2020. COVID-19 has led to cascading crises, each intensifying the next – health, economic, political, racial justice, and environmental – forcing a move to remote teaching. I wonder whether this will be the end of my life as a teacher or possibly the beginning of a new one? It's not only a matter of learning new modes of communication and interaction but abandoning what I have practiced for forty years. I succumb to the use of PowerPoint – clearer to be sure but less alluring than the spontaneous drawing on the board. There's no room to walk around, no patrolling, no provoking, no joking – so my talk speeds up to make up for the loss of connection, of intimacy. There's no knowing if the students follow, except for the lively exchange on "chat." This is a most unusual year, as the pandemic feeds economic crisis that ricochets into political crisis. To be sure, theory is living in the world beyond, but does the medium overpower the message? It's a fundamental transition from the theater created in the lecture hall to the film composed in my study.

Used to marshalling an enclosed space of interacting bodies, I now have to engage and entertain tiny faces, some revealed, some not, on a desktop display. I can only see twenty-five of them at one time, and even then I cannot monopolize their attention. What about the other 150? With so many videos off, I wonder if they are even there. Behind those little squares are human beings in complex situations, struggling amid the unemployed, scrambling for a place of quiet, perhaps homeless, peering into their cell phones or their tablets, the Internet often failing. The inequalities we've been analyzing become part and parcel of learning – not just visible but magnified. Sociology becomes everyone's common sense, but can I take it one step further? In these bleak times can I convince students that another world is possible when they are struggling to survive; when close family members are dying in horrible circumstances, leading students to drop out of school. We dilute the course, give extensions on papers, show as much sympathy as we can. What can we build out of this crisis teaching in which the much-maligned education of the past becomes a utopia? I realize what a privilege it is to extricate students from their lives and have them right there, physically, in front of me, a captive audience.

It's the last throw of the dice. I transform the course by making the two semesters pivot around Du Bois, putting him in dialogue with the Marxist tradition in the first semester and with sociology in the second semester. Does his entry show us the way forward – a sociologist who stretched lived experience to the regional, to the national, and from there to the global, who wrote from the margins, who marched through crisis after crisis, who saw the barbarism of lynching but also the barbarism of European wars to colonize Africa; a sociologist whose social theory had its Durkheimian, Weberian, and Marxist moments, but who transcended them all, driven forward by his engagement with an unjust world as socialist, as Pan-Africanist, as civil rights leader, as journalist, artist, and novelist – public sociologist par excellence. Can he help us reconstruct sociology's foundations to give new visions to a world out of control?

It turned out that Du Bois's entry exploded the course, burst the bounds of Marx, Weber, and Durkheim, undid the imaginary conversations I had developed over forty-three years. His literary genre, his unsystematic theory, his radicalism, his uncompromising public engagement, his outrage at the atrocities of racism, speaks directly to the students and to the times we are living in. I have changed, the students have changed, the university has changed, and the original inspiration of the theory course – Sociology versus Marxism – has run its course. Putting practice to paper is already a bad omen – threatening to petrify what had been open and experimental. I may not have sounded the death knell to living theory, but my version has had its day. It's time to move on. To retool, to start anew.

Conclusion

Biography Meets History

C. Wright Mills famously wrote that sociology lies at the intersection of biography and history. Marx suggested something similar when he wrote that individuals make history but not under conditions of their own choosing. Wrestling with the balance between voluntarism and determinism is difficult in all circumstances, but far more difficult when applied to oneself as one swerves between authoring one's own life and being a victim of forces one doesn't control. Still, I've tried to steer a course between this Scylla and that Charybdis, making sense of what I've been up to in the last fifty years by turning my trajectory through sociology into an object of analysis, and, at the same time, placing it in a wider context.

I began with a naïve view of policy sociology, with the view that sociology has only to propose reform and the world will miraculously follow its command, that knowledge is emancipatory. But I soon discovered that political and economic contexts not only limit what policy measures are possible but also shape the outcome of any particular intervention. Later, instead of expecting others to spontaneously do what was rational, I tried to win them over by making research findings public, encouraging public discussion, what I call *public sociology*. I then realized that promoting public debate, even if it's successful, can generate a barrage of opposition that may co-opt, deflect, or suppress perspectives distasteful to established interests.

My next step was to understand the constellation of interests that conspire to limit social change. I plunged into critical sociology that attended to the seemingly unbridgeable divide between what is and what could be – the dialectic of utopian and anti-utopian thinking. Here I found that critique of the world was not enough; it was also necessary to criticize theories that were blind to alternatives, bad and good – theories that were complacent before the chasm separating reality and potentiality.

The next move, therefore, was to enter professional sociology to advance a theoretical tradition in which what exists is not immoveable but brings about its own destruction, thereby opening possibilities for advancing toward the impossible. That alternative tradition was Marxism – for so long a pariah within the academic world, now carried by a new generation challenging consecrated sociology. We aimed to show that Marxism as a science was as well if not better equipped to explain the world than what we were served up in graduate school. But, as we joined the battle on professional terrains and even had our victories, we began to lose the war, as institutional pressures emerged to sideline critique.

Running into a cul-de-sac, I grasped the professional reins of power – serendipitously handed to me – and returned to the original quest for a better world. Once again embracing public sociology, but now armed with a more sophisticated understanding of its limitations, I examined the context to which it is a response, in which it is received, and within which it is produced. I was bringing sociology to bear on the possibilities of transcending the limitations of the academic world, celebrating those who had taken that path before me.

In returning to the driving force of my own interest in sociology, I also turned to the genesis of the discipline itself, developing a new appreciation of those founding figures whose powerful vision is endangered by sociology's professional turn. Whereas before the point was to vanquish Durkheim and Weber and the traditions they founded, now the point was to elevate them by putting them into dialogue with Marxism. I now looked upon the canon as the source of the deepest truths of sociology: a moral science built on values; the basis for scientific research programs marked by paradigmatic studies; a sensitivity to the sociologist's presence in the world and a theory of history that casts light on the present and on alternative futures, sending the utopian tide of possibility crashing against the anti-utopian rocks of impossibility. For all their flaws, Marx, Weber, and Durkheim remain with us because their ideas transcend the historical moment and geographic site of their production. Even their flaws are an inspiration to push their ideas forward.

Those who worship science for its own sake, who rely on data – big or small, quantitative or qualitative – also make important contributions – but all too often they lose sight of why sociology came into the world. I turned Alfred North Whitehead's claim that "a science that hesitates to forget its founders is lost" on its head. Sociology is at risk of disappearing into a welter of positivism, a minor branch of economics or political science, if we lose sight of our founders. We will be left scattered among the fashions and the fads of the day.

Today sociology is being revitalized by the rediscovery of W. E. B. Du Bois, for so long denied a place in the pantheon. If he secures a permanent place it will not be as a founder of a provincial US sociology, driven by a meticulous empiricism. On the contrary, he abandoned the confines of professional sociology to develop critical, policy, and public sociologies, aimed at an expanding audience, within the academic field and part of the world beyond, across disciplines and across countries. His attention to racial oppression in the context of capitalism led him to a global sociology, and, at the same time, brought reflexivity to the center of sociology – not to question its science but to advance its science. Throughout his extraordinary life Du Bois reflected on how social and political forces had created him and how his sociology never lost hope for a better world. It may turn out that sociology cannot handle his radicalism and will force him back into a corner of professional sociology, but perhaps the crises of today and the movements they generate will instead carry his expansive mantle into the core of the discipline.

If there was ever a sociologist for whom biography and history were entangled, it was Du Bois. But that precept applies to all of us: the trajectory of the sociologist within the sociological field cannot be separated from the transformation of society. In my case, not only the optimism of youth but also the optimism of the times propelled my expeditions to India to study the language problem in university education, to Africa to study Zambianization in the copper mines and student rebellion. This was the era of postcolonial possibilities. Even my exploration of the bases of consent in the American factory was rooted in the presumption that discovering how society reproduced itself would inform strategies for its transformation. It led me to ask: if hegemony is born in the factory in the US, what did that hegemony look like in other advanced capitalist countries? How stable was that hegemony?

By the 1980s, it turned out, deindustrialization was giving rise to the lean and mean regulation of production in advanced capitalism, and hegemony was becoming hegemonic despotism – a rebalancing of coercion and consent. But things were opening up in Eastern Europe. Poland had Solidarity, Hungary had economic reforms, together they offered vistas of democratic socialism. Once again, my optimism had got the better of my sociology, as state socialism was not followed by a new democratic socialism but a peripheral capitalism with its distinctive ailments. So I left Hungary for the Soviet Union where perestroika was fermenting excitement in a formerly grey country. Within a year of my arrival the Soviet Union, too, would crash – the Bolshevik transition to capitalism extinguishing the flame of perestroika. I stayed in Northern Russia for the next decade, watching the economic demise as the market gobbled up production. This was not a great transformation but a great involution.

Traditional Marxism, with its focus on production, couldn't help me understand the logic behind the chaos because industry itself was disappearing. So I turned to Karl Polanyi. His focus on the historical conditions and consequences of a market society gave me the lens to comprehend why the Chinese transition to capitalism nurtured by the party-state was so successful and the Russian transition of wanton destruction was such a disaster. But Polanyi had his limitations. He considered the adoption of market fundamentalism in the nineteenth century to have been a mistake made by following the dangerous utopianism of liberal economics. He was wrong. Marketization was not a *mistake;* it was forced upon humanity by the inexorable logic of capitalism – not once, not twice, but three times. As capitalism is caught between mutually generated crises of overproduction and profitability, so ever-deeper marketization has been the inevitable solution. There is no limit to what can be commodified – from kidneys to carbon emissions, from tweets to everyday life – and these new markets provide outlets both for excess capital and for cheapening production. Counter-movements saved capitalism from the first and second waves of marketization, but the jury is still out as to whether it can be saved a third time, and if so at what cost.

For Polanyi, it was labor, money, and nature – all factors of production – that succumbed to commodification. Commodification – the turning of objects into things that are bought and sold – can be a destructive process. It begins through an often violent expropriation of entities from their integument – kidneys from the body, labor and land from community, money from economic production. For Polanyi the English enclosure movement was the prototype of expropriation – a process that now assumes a global scale. Once commodified, the commodity itself is in danger of losing its use value. The process of commodification renders labor precarious or useless; it contaminates land, air, and water; it turns money into a source of profit rather than a medium of exchange. The market can even expel commodities from exchange; it can turn them into waste, a process we can call ex-commodification. In the Russian transition to capitalism, wage labor disappeared with industry and survival reverted to subsistence, exchange through money dissolved into barter, and land was abandoned – prefiguring the degradation that is spreading across the globe.

Contra Polanyi, protection against the ravages of the market, most prominently through a welfare state and economic planning, was not the future of the planet, but a blip straddling the middle of the twentieth century in advanced capitalism or state socialism. During my fifty years of ethnographic studies I have witnessed the incursion of the market, upending what safety nets there were in country after country – precarity for the vast majority and untold riches for the few. As I circled the globe the transition wrought by third-wave marketization piled wreckage upon wreckage behind me. The Zambian copper mines faced a precipitous decline based on the falling price of copper, finally bringing the Zambian economy to its knees in the 1990s as "structural adjustment" culminated in auctioning off the mines. Allis-Chalmers, and US manufacturing more generally, closed down under bankruptcy in the 1980s, leaving behind an industrial wasteland we know as the rustbelt. Only five years after I set foot in Csepel Auto, Hungary's socialism began to disintegrate; and only five months after I stopped working in Northern Furniture, Russia took the same road. Meanwhile, back home, third-wave marketization was slowly dismantling the public university. The 1960s dream of free education had flown out of the window in a cycle of declining state support and increasing tuition, as universities began employing cost-reducing armies of exploited lecturers; pursuing revenues with the hare-brained schemes of an ever-expanding administrative class; and exchanging short-term, often illusory gains for long-term losses.

As third-wave marketization imposes its grip on the world, it is forging a new set of crises, having destroyed all the levees and ramparts that might protect it from itself. Intersecting and intensifying crises: the ceaseless commodification of the environment leading to climate change and the destruction of water supplies; the unprotected commodification of labor leading to the migration of the destitute and proliferating floods of refugees; the commodification of healthcare that leaves so many defenseless against pandemics; the commodification of knowledge through digital technologies, dominated by Google, Facebook, Microsoft, Apple, and Amazon, speeding up the circulation of commodities and intensifying surveillance. Finance capital is the driver of all these processes: the spurious making of money from money overseeing destruction and waste, ensuring that the stock market floats high even as the productive economy declines. The social movements that emerge out of this maelstrom can be as irrational as the economy to which they react, as popular sentiments are easily whipped up by dictators and lunatics. But underlying it all is third-wave marketization, the monster that is eating away at the social fabric.

Now is the time for sociology to wake up and take a grip on itself, recover its original mission to defend society against an overweening state and out-of-control market, battle the forces of extinction by elaborating visions growing in the interstices of capitalism. It cannot forsake its utopian and anti-utopian commitments: exposing possibilities within limits and thereby expanding the limits of the possible.

Notes

1 In her elaboration of the utopian method, Ruth Levitas (2013) refers to a similar troika: ontological desire, archeological critique, and architectural design. I use archeology in a different way, stressing the excavation of real utopias.
2 Here are some examples: Mona Younis's (2000) comparison of liberation struggles in South Africa and Israel; Gay Seidman's (1994) comparison of working-class movements in South Africa and Brazil; Fareen Parvez's (2017) comparison of the politics of Islam in France and India; Ron Weitzer's (1990) comparison of the transformation of settler states in Zimbabwe and Northern Ireland; Vedat Milor's (1989) comparison of economic planning in Turkey and France; Jim Ron's (2003) comparison of state violence in Israel and Serbia; Soon Kyoung Cho's (1987) comparison of industrial organization in South Korea and California; Michelle Williams's (2008) comparison of the Communist Parties in South Africa and Kerala; Jeff Sallaz's (2009) comparison of the casino industry in South Africa and the US; Jennifer Chun's (2009) comparison of labor organizing in South Korea and California; Ofer Sharone's (2013) comparison of unemployment and job search in Israel and the US; Cinzia Solari's (2017) comparison of Ukrainian migration to Italy and the US; Marcel Paret's (2013) comparison of the politics of precarity in the US and South Africa; Hwa-Jen Liu's (2015) comparison of labor and environmental movements in Taiwan and South Korea; Gabe Hetland's (2015) comparison of participatory democracy in Venezuela and

Peru. As I always say, in sociology, two is a million times bigger than one.

3 After he left Madison, Maurice published a collection of essays by his former students. See Zeitlin (1980).

4 Our first and only joint endeavor in this project was an early article, entitled "Sociological Marxism," which joined an assessment of the history of Marxism, the potentialities of state socialism, and early versions of real utopias (Burawoy and Wright 2003). In a tribute to Erik's life and work I have traced his shift from a scientific Marxism focused on class analysis to a critical Marxism focused on real utopias (Burawoy 2020).

5 The term "ex-commodified" was first coined by Alex Barnard (2016) in his account of the Freegan movement in New York, where they politicized the wastefulness of capitalism by appropriating surplus food left in dumpsters outside supermarkets and restaurants. Freegans lived off the food as well as distributing it among the needy, underlining the enormous waste produced by capitalism. The movement hit hard times when owners started locking up their dumpsters. Capitalism cannot survive if wage laborers have access to an independent source of subsistence, a point underlined in John Steinbeck's *Grapes of Wrath,* where the starving unemployed are denied access to surplus food that is left to rot.

6 The formulations in this chapter developed from the *Universities in Crisis* blog I ran while ISA Vice-President for National Associations. Ideas and data specific to Berkeley are drawn from the BFA's weekly newsletter, *That Was The Week That Was,* that I edited with Celeste Langan for five years, and from various opinion pieces written for the student newspaper, *The Daily Californian.* I learned much from fellow board members, especially Wendy Brown, Celeste Langan, Leslie Salzinger, and James Vernon.

7 My first attempt to outline my theory of the practice of teaching was in a polemical piece that responded to my good friend Alan Sica's lament about the state of theory textbooks (Burawoy 2013). It was followed by an account of my theory course from the standpoint of teaching assistants (Herring et al. 2016).

8 It's not so simple, of course. There's another Smith, laid out in his *The Theory of Moral Sentiments* (1759), who recognizes that human beings are not only self-interested but have an interest in the well-being of others.

References

Alexander, Peter, and Anita Chan. 2004. Does China Have an Apartheid Pass System? *Journal of Ethnic and Migration Studies*, 30(4): 609–29.

Althusser, Louis. 1969. *For Marx*. London: Allen Lane.

Althusser, Louis, and Etienne Balibar. 1970. *Reading Capital*. New York: Pantheon.

Amin, Samir. 1974. *Accumulation on a World Scale*. New York: Monthly Review Press.

Andrews, Abigail. 2018. *Undocumented Politics: Place, Gender, and the Pathways of Mexican Migrants*. Berkeley: University of California Press.

Arrighi, Giovanni. 1967. *The Political Economy of Rhodesia*. The Hague: Mouton.

———. 1970. Labour Supplies in Historical Perspective: A Study of the Proletarianization of the African Peasantry in Rhodesia. *The Journal of Development Studies*, 6(3): 197–234.

Barnard, Alex. 2016. *Freegans: Diving into the Wealth of Food Waste in America*. Minneapolis: University of Minnesota Press.

Bates, Robert. 1971. *Unions, Parties, and Political Development*. New Haven: Yale University Press.

Beauvoir, Simone de. (1949) 1989. *The Second Sex*. New York: Vintage.

Bell, Daniel. 1973. *The Coming of Post-Industrial Society*. New York: Basic Books.

Bellah, Robert, Richard Madsen, William M. Sullivan, Ann Swidler,

218

References

and Steven Tipton. 1985. *Habits of the Heart: Individualism and Commitment in American Life*. Berkeley: University of California Press.

Blalock, Hubert. 1967. *Toward a Theory of Minority-Group Relations*. New York: John Wiley and Sons.

Blauner, Robert. 1972. *Racial Oppression in America*. Berkeley: University of California Press.

Blum, L. 1991. *Between Feminism and Labor: The Significance of the Comparable Worth Movement*. Berkeley: University of California Press.

Bonacich, Edna. 1981. Capitalism and Race Relations in South Africa: A Split Labor Market Analysis. *Political Power and Social Theory*, 2: 239–77. Greenwich, Conn.: JAI Press.

Braverman, Harry. 1974. *Labor and Monopoly Capital*. New York: Monthly Review Press.

Burawoy, Michael. 1972a. *The Colour of Class on the Copper Mines: From African Advancement to Zambianization*. Manchester: Manchester University Press.

———. 1972b. Another Look at the Mineworker. *African Social Research*, 14: 239–87.

———. 1974. Race, Class and Colonialism. *Social and Economic Studies*, 23(4): 521–50.

———. 1976a. The Functions and Reproduction of Migrant Labor: Comparative Material from Southern Africa and the United States. *American Journal of Sociology*, 82(5): 1,050–87.

———. 1976b. Consciousness and Contradiction: A Study of Student Protest in Zambia. *British Journal of Sociology*, 27(1): 78–98.

———. 1979. *Manufacturing Consent: Changes in the Labor Process under Monopoly Capitalism*. Chicago: University of Chicago Press.

———. 1981. The Capitalist State in South Africa: Marxist and Sociological Perspectives on Race and Class. *Political Power and Social Theory*, 2: 279–335.

———. 1985. *The Politics of Production: Factory Regimes under Capitalism and Socialism*. London: Verso.

———. 1989. Harold Wolpe: Doyen of South African Marxists. *Southern African Review of Books*, 2(6): 8–9.

———. 2004. From Liberation to Reconstruction: Theory and Practice in the Life of Harold Wolpe. *Review of African Political Economy*, 102(31): 657–75.

———. 2005. For Public Sociology. *American Sociological Review*, 70(1): 4–28.

———. 2009. *The Extended Case Method: Four Countries, Four*

Decades, Four Great Transformations, and One Theoretical Tradition. Berkeley: University of California Press.

———. 2013. Living Theory. *Contemporary Sociology*, 42(6): 779–83.

———. 2020. A Tale of Two Marxisms: Remembering Erik Olin Wright. *New Left Review*, 121: 66–98.

Burawoy, Michael, Alice Burton, Ann Arnett Ferguson, Kathryn J. Fox, Joshua Gamson, Nadine Gartrell, Leslie Hurst, Charles Kurzman, Leslie Salzinger, Josepha Schiffman, and Shiori Ui. 1991. *Ethnography Unbound.* Berkeley: University of California Press.

Burawoy, Michael, Joseph A. Blum, Sheba George, Zsuzsa Gille, Teresa Gowan, Lynne Haney, Maren Klawiter, Steven H. Lopez, Sean Ó Riain, and Millie Thayer. 2000. *Global Ethnography.* Berkeley: University of California Press.

Burawoy, Michael, and Kathryn Hendley. 1992. Between Perestroika and Privatization: Divided Strategies and Political Crisis in a Soviet Enterprise. *Soviet Studies*, 44(3): 371–402.

Burawoy, Michael, and Jennifer Johnson-Hanks. 2018. *Second Class Citizens: A Survey of Berkeley Lecturers.* Academic Senate Report, University of California, Berkeley.

Burawoy, Michael, and Pavel Krotov. 1992. The Soviet Transition from Socialism to Capitalism: Worker Control and Economic Bargaining in the Wood Industry. *American Sociological Review*, 57(1): 16–38.

———. 1993. The Economic Basis of Russia's Political Crisis. *New Left Review*, 198: 49–70.

Burawoy, Michael, and János Lukács. 1992. *The Radiant Past: Ideology and Reality in Hungary's Road to Capitalism.* Chicago: University of Chicago Press.

Burawoy, Michael, and Theda Skocpol (eds.) 1983. *Marxist Inquiries: Studies of Labor, Class and States.* Chicago: University of Chicago Press. Supplement to the *American Journal of Sociology*.

Burawoy, Michael, and Erik Wright. 2003. Sociological Marxism. Pp. 459–86 in Jonathan Turner (ed.), *The Handbook of Sociological Theory*. New York: Plenum Books.

Carey, Alex. 1967. The Hawthorne Studies: A Radical Criticism. *American Sociological Review*, 37: 403–16.

Castells, Manuel. 1975. Immigrant Workers and Class Struggles in Advanced Capitalism: The Western European Experience. *Politics and Society*, 5(1): 33–66.

Chang, Andy Scott. Forthcoming. Selling a Resume and Buying a Job: Stratification of Gender and Occupation by States and Brokers in International Migration from Indonesia. *Social Problems.*

Cho, Soon Kyoung. 1987. *How Cheap Is "Cheap Labor"? The Dilemmas of Export Industrialization.* PhD dissertation, University of California, Berkeley.

Chuang, Julia. 2020. *Beneath the China Boom: Labor, Citizenship, and the Making of a Rural Land Market.* Oakland: University of California Press.

Chun, Jennifer. 2009. *Organizing at the Margins: The Symbolic Politics of Labor in South Korea and the United States.* Ithaca, N.Y.: Cornell University Press.

Collins, Patricia Hill. 1986. Learning from the Outsider Within: The Sociological Significance of Black Feminist Thought. *Social Problems,* 33(6): S14–S32.

Connell, R. W. 1997. Why Is Classical Theory Classical? *American Journal of Sociology,* 102(6): 1511–57.

Cottom, Tressie McMillan. 2017. *Lower Ed: The Troubling Rise of For-Profit Colleges in the New Economy.* New York: New Press.

Davies, Robert, David Kaplan, Mike Morris, and Dan O'Meara. 1976. Class Struggle and Periodization of the State in South Africa. *Review of African Political Economy,* 3(7): 4–30.

Desmond, Matthew. 2016. *Evicted: Poverty and Property in the American City.* New York: Crown Books.

Du Bois, W. E. B. (1896) 2007. *The Suppression of the African Slave-Trade to the United States of America, 1638–1870.* New York: Oxford University Press.

———. 1899. *The Philadelphia Negro.* Philadelphia: University of Pennsylvania Press.

———. (1903) 1989. *The Souls of Black Folk.* London and New York: Penguin Books.

———. (1909) 1996. *John Brown.* New York: Monthly Review Press.

———. (1911) 2007. *The Quest of the Silver Fleece.* New York: Oxford University Press.

———. (1920) 1999. *Darkwater: Voices from Within the Veil.* New York: Dover.

———. (1928) 2007. *Dark Princess.* New York: Oxford University Press.

———. (1935) 1998. *Black Reconstruction in America, 1860–1880.* New York: Free Press.

———. (1940) 2007. *Dusk of Dawn: An Essay Toward an Autobiography of a Race Concept.* New York: Oxford University Press.

———. (1947) 2007. *The World and Africa: An Inquiry into the Part which Africa has played in World History.* New York: Oxford University Press.

Durkheim, Émile. (1893) 2014. *The Division of Labor in Society*. New York: Free Press.

———. (1897) 1997. *Suicide*. New York: Free Press.

Fanon, Frantz. (1961) 1968. *The Wretched of the Earth*. New York: Grove Weidenfeld.

Ferguson, James. 1994. *The Anti-Politics Machine: "Development," Depoliticization and Bureaucratic Power in Lesotho*. New York: Cambridge University Press.

Feyerabend, Paul. 1975. *Against Method*. London: New Left Books.

Frank, Andre Gunder. 1966. *Development of Underdevelopment*. New York: Monthly Review Press.

Franke, Richard H., and James D. Kaul. 1978. The Hawthorne Experiments: First Statistical Interpretation. *American Sociological Review*, 43: 623–43.

Fuller, Linda. 1992. *Work and Democracy in Socialist Cuba*. Philadelphia: Temple University Press.

George, Sheba. 2005. *When Women Come First: Gender and Class in Transnational Migration*. Berkeley: University of California Press.

Gitlin, Todd. 1980. *The Whole World Is Watching: Mass Media in the Making and Unmaking of the New Left*. Berkeley: University of California Press.

Glaser, Barney, and Anselm Strauss. 1967. *The Discovery of Grounded Theory*. Chicago: Aldine.

Gouldner, Alvin. 1970. *The Coming Crisis of Western Sociology*. New York: Basic Books.

Government of the Republic of Zambia. 1968. *The Progress of Zambianization in the Mining Industry*. Lusaka: Government Printer.

Gramsci, Antonio. 1971. *Selections from the Prison Notebooks*. New York: International Publishers.

Hamilton, Laura, and Kelly Nielsen. 2021. *Broke: The Racial Consequences of Underfunding Public Universities*. Chicago: University of Chicago Press.

Hammond, J. L., and Barbara Hammond. 1911. *The Village Labourer, 1760–1832: A Study in the Government of England before the Reform Bill*. London: Longmans, Green and Co.

———. 1917. *The Town Labourer, 1760–1832, The New Civilization*. London: Longmans, Green and Co.

Hanafi, Sari. 2011. University Systems in the Arab East: Publish Globally and Perish Locally vs. Publish Locally and Perish Globally. *Current Sociology*, 59(3): 291–309.

Haraszti, Miklós. 1977. *A Worker in a Worker's State*. Harmondsworth: Penguin Books.

Harvey, David. 2003. *The New Imperialism*. New York: Oxford University Press.

Herring, Chris, Manuel Rosaldo, Josh Seim, and Benjamin Shestakofsky. 2016. Living Theory: Principles and Practices for Teaching Social Theory Ethnographically. *Teaching Sociology*, 44(3): 188–99.

Hetland, Gabriel. 2015. *Making Democracy Real: Participatory Governance in Urban Latin America*. PhD dissertation, University of California, Berkeley.

Hochschild, Arlie. 1989. *The Second Shift: Working Parents and the Revolution at Home*. New York: Viking Books.

———. 2016. *Strangers in Their Own Land*. New York: New Press.

Hondagneu-Sotelo, Pierrette. 1994. *Gendered Transitions: Mexican Experiences of Immigration*. Berkeley: University of California Press.

Iskander, Natasha. 2010. *Creative State: Forty Years of Migration and Development Policy in Morocco and Mexico*. Ithaca, N.Y.: Cornell University Press.

Jameson, Fredric. 2003. Future City. *New Left Review*, 21: 65–79.

Jencks, Christopher, and David Riesman. 1968. *The Academic Revolution*. New York: Doubleday.

Johnston, Paul. 1994. *Success While Others Fail: Social Movement Unionism and the Public Workplace*. Ithaca, N.Y.: Cornell University Press.

Kerr, Clark. 1963. *The Uses of the University*. Cambridge, Mass.: Harvard University Press.

Konrád, George and Iván Szelényi. 1979. *The Intellectuals on the Road to Class Power*. New York: Harcourt Brace Jovanovich.

Kuhn, Thomas. 1962. *The Structure of Scientific Revolutions*. Chicago: University of Chicago Press.

Lakatos, Imre. 1978. *The Methodology of Scientific Research Programmes*. Cambridge: Cambridge University Press.

Lee, Ching Kwan. 1998. *Gender and the South China Miracle*. Berkeley: University of California Press.

Lenin, Vladimir Ilyich Ulyanov. (1917) 1975. State and Revolution. Pp. 311–98 in Robert Tucker (ed.), *The Lenin Anthology*. New York: Norton.

Levitas, Ruth. 2013. *Utopia as Method*. London: Palgrave Macmillan.

Liu, Hwa-Jen. 2015. *Leverage of the Weak: Labor and Environmental Movements in Taiwan and South Korea*. Minneapolis: University of Minnesota Press.

Lopez, Steven. 2004. *Reorganizing the Rust Belt: An Inside Study of the American Labor Movement*. Berkeley: University of California Press.

Luker, Kristin. 1984. *Abortion and the Politics of Motherhood.* Berkeley: University of California Press.

MacKinnon, Catharine. 1982. Feminism, Marxism, Method and the State: An Agenda for Theory. *Signs,* 7(3): 515–44.

Milkman, Ruth. 1987. *Gender at Work: The Dynamics of Job Segregation by Sex during World War II.* Champaign: University of Illinois Press.

———. 2020. *Immigrant Labor and the New Precariat.* Cambridge, UK: Polity Press.

Mill, John Stuart. 1888. *A System of Logic.* New York: Harper, Eighth Edition.

Mills, Charles Wright. 1948. *New Men of Power.* New York: Harcourt Brace.

———. 1951. *White Collar.* New York: Oxford University Press.

———. 1956. *The Power Elite.* New York: Oxford University Press.

———. 1959. *The Sociological Imagination.* New York: Oxford University Press.

Milor, Vedat. 1989. *The Comparative Study of Planning and Economic Development in Turkey and France.* PhD dissertation, University of California, Berkeley.

Moore, Barrington. 1966. *Social Origins of Dictatorship and Democracy: Lords and Peasant in the Making of the Modern World.* Boston: Beacon.

Morris, Aldon. 2015. *The Scholar Denied: W. E. B. Du Bois and the Birth of Modern Sociology.* Oakland: University of California Press.

Mouffe, Chantal. 2018. *For a Left Populism.* London: Verso.

Newfield, Christopher. 2008. *Unmaking the Public University: The Forty Year Assault on the Middle Class.* Cambridge, Mass.: Harvard University Press.

———. 2016. *The Great Mistake: How We Wrecked Public Universities and How We Can Fix Them.* Baltimore: Johns Hopkins University Press.

Paige, Jeffrey. 1975. *Agrarian Revolution: Social Movements and Export Agriculture in the Underdeveloped World.* New York: Free Press.

Paret, Marcel. 2011. Borders and Exploitation: Migrant Labor Systems in California and South Africa. *Berkeley Journal of Sociology,* 55: 57–96.

———. 2013. *Precarious Politics: Working Class Insecurity and Struggles for Recognition in the United States and South Africa, 1994–2010.* PhD dissertation, University of Chicago.

Parsons, Talcott. 1937. *The Structure of Social Action.* Two volumes. New York: McGraw-Hill.

————. 1950. The Prospects of Sociological Theory. *American Sociological Review*, 15(1): 3–16.

Parvez, F. 2017. *Politicizing Islam: The Islamic Revival in France and India*. New York: Oxford University Press.

Polanyi, Karl. 1944. *The Great Transformation*. Boston: Beacon Books.

Polanyi, Michael. 1958. *Personal Knowledge*. London: Routledge and Kegan Paul.

Popper, Karl. 1963. *Conjectures and Refutations: The Growth of Scientific Knowledge*. London: Routledge and Kegan Paul.

Poulantzas, Nicos. 1973. *Political Power and Social Classes*. London: Verso.

Przeworski, Adam. 1985. *Capitalism and Social Democracy*. New York: Cambridge University Press.

Ray, Raka. 2017. A Case of Internal Colonialism? Arlie Hochschild's *Strangers in Their Own Land*. *British Journal of Sociology*, 68(1): 129–33.

Rodney, Walter. 1972. *How Europe Underdeveloped Africa*. London: Bogle-L'Ouverture Publications.

Rodriguez, Robyn. 2010. *Migrants for Export: How the Philippine State Brokers Labor to the World*. Minneapolis: University of Minnesota Press.

Roethlisberger, Fritz Jules, and Dickson, William. 1939. *Management and the Worker*. Cambridge, MA: Harvard University Press.

Ron, James. 2003. *Frontiers and Ghettos: State Violence in Serbia and Israel*. Berkeley: University of California Press.

Roy, Donald. 1952. *Restriction of Output in a Piecework Machine Shop*. PhD dissertation, University of Chicago.

Sallaz, Jeffrey. 2009. *The Labor of Luck: Casino Capitalism in the United States and South Africa*. Berkeley: University of California Press.

Salzinger, Leslie. 2003. *Genders in Production*. Berkeley: University of California Press.

Samuels, Robert. 2013. *Why Public Higher Education Should Be Free*. New Brunswick, NJ: Rutgers University Press.

Sánchez-Jankowski, Martín. 1991. *Islands in the Street: Gangs and American Urban Society*. Berkeley: University of California Press.

Seidman, Gay. 1994. *Manufacturing Militance: Workers' Movements in Brazil and South Africa, 1970–1985*. Berkeley: University of California Press.

Seim, Joshua. 2020. *Bandage, Sort, and Hustle*. Berkeley: University of California Press.

————. Forthcoming. Participant Observation, Observant

Participation, and Hybrid Ethnography. *Sociological Methods & Research*.

Sharone, Ofer. 2013. *Flawed System/Flawed Self: Job Searching and Unemployment Experiences*. Chicago: University of Chicago Press.

Sherman, Rachel. 2007. *Class Acts: Service and Inequality in Luxury Hotels*. Berkeley: University of California Press.

Simons, Jack, and Ray Simons. 1969. *Class and Colour in South Africa, 1850–1950*. Harmondsworth: Penguin Books.

Skocpol, Theda. 1979. *States and Social Revolutions: A Comparative Analysis of France, Russia, and China*. New York: Cambridge University Press.

Smith, Adam. (1759) 2010. *The Theory of Moral Sentiments*. London: Penguin Books.

———. (1776) 1976. *An Inquiry into the Nature and Causes of the Wealth of Nations*. Chicago: University of Chicago Press.

Solari, Cinzia. 2017. *On the Shoulders of Grandmothers: Gender, Migration, and Post-Soviet Nation-State Building*. New York: Routledge.

Staniszkis, Jadwiga. 1984. *Poland's Self-Limiting Revolution*. Princeton: Princeton University Press.

Szelényi, Iván. 1983. *Urban Social Inequalities Under State Socialism*. Oxford: Oxford University Press.

Tucker, Robert (ed.) 1978. *The Marx–Engels Reader*. New York: Norton.

Van Velsen, Jaap. 1960. Labour Migration as a Positive Factor in the Continuity of Tonga Tribal Society. *Economic Development and Cultural Change*, 8: 265–78.

———. 1964. *The Politics of Kinship*. Manchester: Manchester University Press.

———. 1967. The Extended Case Method and Situational Analysis. Pp. 29–53 in A. L. Epstein (ed.), *The Craft of Urban Anthropology*. London: Tavistock.

Wallerstein, Immanuel. 1974. *The Modern World-System I*. New York: Academic Press.

Weber, Max. (1904–5, 1920) 1958. *The Protestant Ethic and the Spirit of Capitalism*. New York: Charles Scribner's Sons.

———. (1917) 1994. Science as a Vocation. Pp. 129–156 in H. H. Gerth and C. W. Mills, from *Max Weber: Essays in Sociology*. New York: Oxford University Press.

———. (1919) 1994. Politics as a Vocation. Pp. 77–128 in H. H. Gerth and C. W. Mills, from *Max Weber: Essays in Sociology*. New York: Oxford University Press.

Weitzer, Ron. 1990. *Transforming Settler States: Communal Conflict and Internal Security in Northern Ireland and Zimbabwe*. Berkeley: University of California Press.

Williams, Michelle. 2008. *The Roots of Participatory Democracy: Democratic Communists in South Africa and Kerala, India.* London: Palgrave Macmillan.

Wilson, William Julius. 1973. *Power, Racism, and Privilege: Race Relations in Theoretical and Sociohistorical Perspectives.* New York: Free Press.

———. 1978. *The Declining Significance of Race: Blacks and Changing American Institutions.* Chicago: University of Chicago Press.

———. 1987. *The Truly Disadvantaged: The Inner City, the Underclass, and Public Policy.* Chicago: University of Chicago Press.

———. 1996. *When Work Disappears: The World of the New Urban Poor.* New York: Knopf.

Wolpe, Harold. 1972. Capitalism and Cheap Labour-Power in South Africa: From Segregation to Apartheid. *Economy and Society,* 1(4): 425–56.

Wright, Erik Olin. 1979. *Class Structure and Income Determination.* New York: Academic Press.

———. 1985. *Classes.* London and New York: Verso.

———. 1987. Reflections on *Classes. Berkeley Journal of Sociology,* 32: 19–49.

———. 1997. *Class Counts: Comparative Studies in Class Analysis.* New York: Cambridge University Press.

———. 2010. *Envisioning Real Utopias.* London and New York: Verso.

———. 2019. *How To Be an Anticapitalist in the 21st Century.* London and New York: Verso.

———. 2020. *Stardust to Stardust: Reflections on Living and Dying.* Chicago: Haymarket Books.

Younis, Mona. 2000. *Liberation and Democratization: The South African and Palestinian National Movements.* Minneapolis: University of Minnesota Press.

Zeitlin, Maurice. 1980. *Classes, Class Conflict, and the State.* Cambridge, Mass.: Winthrop Publishers.

Zuboff, Shoshana. 2019. *The Age of Surveillance Capitalism: The Fight for a Human Future at the New Frontier of Power.* New York: Public Affairs.

Index